D0335256

Gardening Down a Rabbit Hole

Gardening Down a Rabbit Hole

Josephine Saxton

AIDAN ELLIS

TO MGF, who for mysterious
reasons of his own, wishes to
remain anonymous

First published in the United Kingdom by
Aidan Ellis Publishing, Cobb House, Nuffield,
Henley on Thames, Oxon RG9 5RT

First edition 1996

Illustrations: Josephine Howard

A CIP catalogue record for this book is available from the
British Library

Filmset by Contour Typesetters, Southall, Middx UB2 4BD
Printed in England by Biddles Ltd, Guildford,
Surrey GU1 1DA

ISBN: 0 85628 282 0

Contents

	Foreword	1
1	Gardening Down a Rabbit Hole	6
2	How Not to Begin	20
3	How It Began	29
4	Out and About with MGF	46
5	Light and Shade	65
6	Tearing Away the Veil	80
7	Paradise on Earth	92
8	The Mystery Plant	101
9	A Craze for Blue	114
10	Derry & Tom's?	129
11	Rain or Shine	140
12	Turning Pro	153
13	Receiving Admiration	165
14	The Plagues of Egypt	177
15	Further Initiations	197
16	Gullibility	216
	Appendices	231

Foreword

I am writing this foreword after I have finished the rest of the book, which in rabbit hole land makes perfect sense: how else would I know what I had written about? By all means read it at the end, otherwise how will you know what I mean?

I bought a mirror today. It was pure intuition setting out to buy it, I had decided to wait until next spring for this, which really means autumn because I can never wait sensibly if I am in the grip of an idea. I set off this afternoon and followed my nose until there it was, leaning against the doorpost of a junkshop, just the right size and already drilled for fixing. The man will deliver it at tea-time, for a total of twelve pounds. It will be fixed, I think with one or more strong men to assist, on the shady north wall of Wonderland, behind a Japanese *Acer palmatum* 'Dissectum Atropurpureum' which will be lovingly planted in the tub which now contains a fuchsia surplus to requirements. Space will appear, and then it will be Through the Looking Glass as well. I shall wish I had more of these mirrors, there were sets of them and they had all come from a hairdresser's shop. What good luck!

It goes on and on, this little garden, and if I fix another mirror opposite the first, it will be infinite. It is an idea worth considering. Any idea you have for a

garden is worth considering, because if it is successful the rewards are enormous. The bench has been
moved across the gate and there is just room between
that and a large pot of bamboo to get in and out. J
does not live here any more, he can sit in the sun and
read his papers elsewhere I do not doubt. Where the
bench was there is, just as I dreamed, an enormous
dahlia, an interesting dark red rush in a pot and a
Juncus effusus which spirals about like something
from another planet. And behind them, ivy and the
impossibly placed roots of a *Passiflora caerulea*.
Then comes the new deeper, but still narrow, flower
bed which I built up from old bricks found behind
and under things, topped off with some wavy edging
slabs, now hidden by foliage. Filling that was a bit of
bother, in between snow storms for allowing the
cement to harden I dashed out for yet another couple
of sacks of compost and composted horse manure
until I was exhausted, several big hauling trips. It is
incredible how many bags of compost will disappear
into even a tiny raised bed. I regret to say that
afterwards I was not at all well, but hardly noticed
this, I was so excited about mixing cement, making a
good job of the bricklaying, filling it in and planting
it. Lovely way to spend a freezing February week-
end. The lilies in that border were perfect, the sweet
peas less so. Sweet peas against a wall covered in
leafy climbers do not really thrive, this is the third
year when they have given up the ghost too soon. The
Sedum spectabile is enormous and will flower any
moment now, so there will be good colour against
the dark green ivy.

I remember that bed the first couple of years. It

2

was sparse, dry, rather pathetic. A thick patch of nicotiana saved it, but it held no promise at all. Now there will be something interesting in there at all times of year. In the corner which was once impossibly dank and difficult there are three ferns, an enormous orange flowered begonia, a small white fuchsia, a pot of striped grass (*Glyceria maxima* 'Variegata'), and other kinds of pendulous begonias so that hardly anything but living growth is discernible. The enormous icy pink rose is flowering for the second time this year, and has earned its keep as a guard-rose. One night I awoke to hear some crashing, a howl of pain and curses followed by running feet. It was like the Goon Show and I laughed aloud. Another foiled thief! I had pruned that rose and been shredded, and knew the pain it can cause. I hope he had his anti-tetanus injections.

All the foxgloves but one (in a dark corner by the french doors under a fern by the root of the *Hedera helix*) have gone. I am finally of the opinion that their lower leaves are too large for a small space, they block the light from other plants too much. But the alstroemeria were marvellous this year, and they were the ones which I tipped out of a pot thinking they were dead but should have another chance. They could become a nuisance, I am told. Good luck to them. The 'Aloha' rose is thriving, offering a couple of second flowers, and the 'F.H. Young' clematis is also flowering for a second time, twining itself around next door's *Fuchsia magellanica*, its blue (mauve) flowers contrasting prettily with the fuchsia flowers and a few late honeysuckle flowers and red berries.

Across the path not more than two feet away, the leaves from the pot of montbretia have turned a fabulous pale orange colour, and the sage next door is showing new leaf after I pruned it after flowering. Two rather common plants giving yet another uncommon colour combination; in the changing light of a grey afternoon shot with optimistic shafts of sunlight, this is exhilarating. The dankest and most difficult shady spots are full of enormous white begonia flowers and shiny spears of leaves of the *Iris foetidissima*, which will show startling pods of scarlet berries when the first frost arrives. All the Japanese anemones, both those donated by MGF three years ago and a pot I bought at Cotswold Garden Flowers (Badsey near Evesham, a marvellous place to over-spend), and their pale pink flowers lighten up the space above several different ferns. That sub-tropical fern which I found on the compost heap in Jephson Gardens is marvellous now, in a large pot of its own, with dozens of elegant long striped leaves. The *Abutilon megapotamicum* 'Variegata' is still in full flower with masses of dazzling leafy branches.

My new rose is thriving by the french doors, and the nepeta which MGF almost caused me to kill by demanding half its root is back with redoubled strength. I do not know what became of his half but I never saw it in S's garden when I was working there. Very sad, but there will be a purple haze good enough for Jimi Hendrix by my door next spring, and it will look lovely near some white and blue hyacinths, an oddly artificial-looking flower which I have learned to love, at last.

It is all very different from my original ideas and

plantings, and quite the best year yet. It is of course chronically overcrowded, but I now have the technique of passing on plants which do not thrive here, or which I am tired of, so that I can make room for something newly discovered. The orange azalea was passed on yet again after its recipient moved house, and I saw it last week, a thriving bush with which she was delighted in spring when it flowered massively. But now owner number three needs to find it a new home because her colour scheme is to be creams and yellows.

Just occasionally I get a longing for a space of utter simplicity. I would have one or two rocks, beautifully raked gravel, the Japanese maple and the mirror and a few choice alpines. And a small bubbling spring to aid peaceful contemplation. I sometimes feel like that about the rooms in the house. A futon, a cupboard, one exquisite paper lantern, a bonsai. But really, this is not for me, I love certain pieces of furniture and rugs too much for that, and all plants.

I have just done a mental count, and there are approximately three hundred and sixty plants in that small back yard. I make no apology nor excuse for this excess, nor boast of the success. The present result was only come to by trial and error, and rather a large number of those tiresome plants of the family *procumbens mortei*.

I do say that if you love plants and have only a tiny space, you can have a garden of your own.

Josephine Saxton (Howard)
1996

1

Gardening Down a Rabbit Hole

There are no rabbits in this book. Nor moles nor
deer. All other garden pests known to horticulturalists of all genres emerge in due season, but
my present garden is so small that if a rabbit
managed to get in it wouldn't eat anything; it would
die of acute claustrophobia. And there is, of course,
no lawn for a mole to landscape, and deer are
completely out of the question. The garden is a
typical patch at the back of a Victorian terrace-
house, pretentiously described by an estate agent
as an artisan's cottage. Is an obsessive gardener
an artisan? Who knows these things any more,
gardeners are everywhere now, it is a national craze.
I have always been subject to it, but only in recent
years has the disease set in chronically.

Now, the house itself, although the subject of
intensive housepride and a haven from turmoil, is the
shelter in front of the important part of the property,
which to many is the yard outside where a bike may
be half sheltered in an outside loo. I now feel strongly
that a dwelling without a garden is a trap, not a
home. The garden is an extra outdoor sitting-room,
in which the décor constantly changes, sometimes to
your own design and sometimes, of course, definitely
not.

My longest continual bit of earth is just over nine

metres long, and that is only half a metre wide. Hardly worth writing a book about, one might think. In that case, add another strip of two and three quarter metres by twenty-six centimetres, plus two half metre squares made by prising up bricks, and a very small planter built against the kitchen wall. Everything else is in pots and tubs and cracks. There is a considerable amount of growth now, an example of the small paradise which glows inside every gardener's mind. I thought as a child that I would like to be a gypsy, a wanderer, an explorer or traveller. My Granma's brother disappeared aged twelve to become a tramp, so the story goes, and was never heard from again. I always thought he must have had a wonderful life. But now I pity him. No garden!

Clearly I am not in spirit a hunter-gatherer, but a settler, after all. I must have my bit of land staked out and things growing on it or I feel dispossessed, literally unsettled. I haven't taken holidays in two years, not only because I have spent all my money on plants and other garden necessities, but because I cannot possibly trust anyone else to feed and water it all properly in my absence. I would not know a moment's relaxation, for thinking about drooping nicotiana, shrivelled petunias, panting roses and untrained clematis and sweet peas. What if I returned to crisp ferns? What if the gentians were watered with limey town water instead of rain or filtered? Dead penstemons to greet me during jetlag! I would die too.

I once went away for a week leaving a person in charge who simply did not water at all, and that in baking weather. I left no instructions it is true, I just took it for granted that the person knew about these things; being quite a heavy drinker should confer understanding of libation. Lots of plants died, and so did the friendship. This incident was not the first intimation that all was not quite good about the person in question, but to me it confirmed some feelings of disquiet which I had nobly put to one side. One can simply not ever feel right about people who behave like that towards what are, after all, a much more important life form than human beings. This is one of the first precepts of gardening, if there are to be any at all. Plants are alive, and very important in the scheme of things. It is a privilege to look after them.

It has taken me almost seven years, a great deal of time, pain and money, this patch of mine, before such an idea began to dawn upon me. I wasn't gardening just to give myself thrills and a show of colour, there was more to it than that, gratifying as it all is. I know profoundly that everything has been worthwhile.

How could such a small garden take up so many resources? Well, I garden down the rabbit hole in Alice in Wonderland, or inside the Tardis, or through the door in the Faery Mountain, where everything is bigger on the inside than the outside. And I have learned gardening the hard way, by trial and error, against all odds. Love of plants was not enough to get them to grow. Only to a limited extent will a plant thrive if it is not getting what its genetic structure demands. Many can adapt extensively, but many simply die. This may be glaringly obvious to most gardeners but it wasn't to me. When it began to sink into my dense grey matter was when my gardening improved. If it was not so crammed, so overflowing, so English, my garden would be a Zen garden, teaching me secrets just by existing. It will doubtless continue to teach me as the years go by, should I resist the temptation to buy an old field and garden that, living the while in a tent.

And this enterprise also took imagination. I have an infinite and very eclectic quantity of that, an attribute which has not always been an advantage but which has finally paid off. An excess amounting to megalomania has led me to terrible disasters, crises, impasses and almost despair. I have never been quite as unrealistic in this small space as a woman I know with a similar small space who has recently planted a gunnera, which will eventually reach four metres tall and probably larger across, is poisonous and needs a large bog to thrive; but I have been quite unreasonable, sometimes with good results for a while. For example when I believed it might be possible to overwinter pelargoniums for-ever, simply because they had done well for two winters, very mild ones. Fake Mediterranean growth had elided the memory of hard frosts, which kill some things within hours. Including my 'Elégantes', a metre in length, growing in chimney pots. Much loved, sadly mourned.

But this is what gardening is all about. Total identification with the glorious scene painted on the Internet of your mind, which will also change radically with every great garden you visit, with every garden book you read, and with every new nursery or garden centre in which you find yourself, wherever you go. If you have the slightest interest in plants and a bit of plastic on you, it is unsafe to go out now, the trap is sprung everywhere. Just as you think you are clear, driving along in the middle of nowhere, a garden centre or plant nursery sign springs up and before you know it you are that bit further into overdraft.

At one time we got plants from neighbours, Woolworth's and the local greengrocer. We gathered horse manure after the coal and the milkman's horses, dug in some soot after the sweep had been, all at very little expense. Those days are past. We are no longer allowed even to sprout a few seeds on the windowsill, we are told that we need an electrically warmed propagator, a greenhouse, a conservatory, a small fortune! Not all true, of course. You will also need a passion for plants bordering on mania, the stamina of a mountaineer and an eagerness to learn more usually found in highly intelligent seven-year-old children.

When I first began this condensed Eden I thought I knew a great deal about horticulture, having created seven different gardens and then moved on, not always from choice. There was a time when married women upped tent-pegs when their husbands got better jobs elsewhere, no matter how much they liked where they already were. Not only did one's own career, if any, go down the drain, the gardens were heartlessly sold from under one's wellies. This smallest of all my gardens (but it *is* all mine) has been the most difficult, and it is my best production so far. If you have very little earth, a poor aspect and a hostile climate, even there you can make a garden, and much quicker than I did if you make the right beginnings. Don't just look at gardens and books on the subject; study them, take notes, decide what you love. It is also a great advantage to acquire a Gardening Friend much more experienced in horticulture than yourself.

When a severe illness gave me three months with nothing to do but recover, My Gardening Friend and I spent a lot of time visiting wonderful gardens. We worked our way through as much of the National Garden Society handbook and the National Trust as we could, he lecturing knowledgeably all the way, and me asking questions and soaking in the replies as if I had to pass an exam.

He is an interesting person, whom I shall refer to as MGF, a vast store of knowledge about plantlife. Walk down a garden path with him and you take several senior members of the Royal Horticultural Society with you, not to mention the ghosts of such luminaries as the Tradescants, Linnaeus, Fortune, Douglas and Darwin, and several others including Gertrude Jekyll, the genius who discovered that there is no law against standing a successful pot of flowers in an unsuccessful spot in the border.

MGF is self-trained, but seems to know about

almost any growing thing you can point to, its species, genus, origins, botanical name, who discovered it and when, what soil and conditions it prefers and in what other forms it might be found. Visiting gardens with him is an illuminating experience. So in him I have been fortunate, although he is also rather bossy, as I shall relate, and always seems to get the idea that any garden he helps with belongs to him and, therefore, the owner should not interfere. It has taken me many fierce battles to get him to respect my ownership of my own patch, but some of my ancestors owned castles, so I am told, and I inherit a defence system which no marauder can breach.

Passiflora cerulea.

I almost did not forgive him handling my sole fruit on a *Passiflora caerulea* thus causing it to drop off.

'Oh it will seed itself if you just wash it into a crack,' he said airily, his long hands waving about dismissively, and indeed this has proved to be the case. The new seedling is two metres tall, growing in nothing at the back of my small garden bench. My forgiveness preceded many more garden visits, for which I am grateful.

Years ago I hadn't been to any great gardens, or if I had I never noticed them as gardens. They were simply blobs of colour and wafts of scent to enhance my days out visiting the great houses. Hence my utterly negative reaction to the Boboli Gardens in Florence. Not a flower in sight, just a lot of Italian architecture, dry grass, dusty bushes, steps, and grit to fill my already hellish straw sandals which I had purchased in the Firenze market thinking they would be ideal for sightseeing. But as for *garden* per se, I've had much more ecstatic horticultural experiences as a child in the People's Park, Halifax, Yorks.

That northern miracle has much exotic colour, most of it rhododendron because of the acid soil. This a creature I have become intensely cautious of since my daughter, an ecologist, related to me the damage they do to the environment. One rhododendron can put roots underground and shoot up babies for three square miles, and be almost impossible to shift before it permanently ruins the soil it despoils. Marvellously exotic flowers, of course, which should never have been imported from the foothills of the Himalayas or China. I have no rhododendron, not even its New World cousin a small azalea, needless to say, in my small patch. I gave away my last azalea last year, twisted and non-floral from its confinement in a tub of coir under an enthusiastic cabbagey ivy, but looking like an exotic spiralling bonsai. It had been fed with tealeaves and love and sequestered iron but it was still as miserable as sin. A new owner with an acid soil patch and a more open space has it now; she is Scottish and instantly loved its pale leaves, and she will have it showing off its orange blobs very soon. I have outgrown azaleas; they are vulgar at best. This is a stage, says MGF, through which all gardeners must pass, from the utterly obvious to the marvellously interesting.

I did not enjoy the Boboli, only the view from a terrace. I am not a landscaper, I am a plantsperson, it would seem, unless the ability to balance one plant-pot on top of another and get it to work, visually and practically, is landscaping. More like painting, really, which is another of my *raisons d'être*, or should that be *bêtes noires*?

Ethnographers (me and MGF) classify early people into first Nomads and Settlers, and then into Builders and Agriculturalists. An obsessed plants-person gardener is probably a bearer of genes from both Settlers and Agriculturalists. Neither MGF nor myself are genetically related to any New Age Traveller or Capability Brown, neither of whom are famous for training roses to come right into the drawing-room, which I once did, caring more about rose scent than security. We admire from a distance these vast steps towards a primitive past and a sculptured future. And as for the well-documented Italian scorn of English architecture and gardening, in which flowers in window-boxes have been declared an eyesore – pfui! or whatever Italians say. They do not live under a grey blanket like most of the British do, and cannot perhaps appreciate sufficiently what flowers can do for the human spirit on a bleak island. I noticed a mirror glass skyscraper from the train recently, its stark lines spoiled completely by various window-boxes. I could have cheered, much as I do when I find moss growing in the grooves on my car. To me this signifies an important triumph of nature.

If they let me loose in the Boboli I would have clematis and roses twining all around those classic balustrades, florid planters on every plinth, palms shading the pathways and acres of flowering trees lushly underplanted with exotic bulbs.

There are of course many other fabulous gardens in Italy, but many of them are based on the traditional English pattern, with the added advantage of much sunshine. In the cities, the gardens are secret, on rooftops and balconies, out of sight, rather like my own, again with more sun. The British Isles, in which for garden purposes I include the Republic of Ireland, have most of the finest gardens in the world. Most flowers grown in these islands were introduced from elsewhere, like most of its human inhabitants have always been. The proportion of native plants is about the same as true historical natives, which is precisely why we have not only the best and most varied gardens, but the most exciting music and culture, despite being famous for

15

xenophobia. That, I believe, springs from a fear that yet more incomers will take from us what we already have, instead of which, of course, they always add to it. Imagine a Britain descended only from a few Stone Age hunters! Our plant-list would be very sparse and boring, and inbred too.

Most of our best 'English' gardens are filled with plants which are Chinese, Antipodean, African, South American and Indian, indeed from almost everywhere. Sailors, botanists and explorers brought them back, invaders brought plants with them. (The Romans brought that marauding mollusc the voracious garden snail, which we will never be rid of.) Plants were painted, studied, cultivated, adopted, presumed to be native and now the garden centres cash in. Examine an average hanging basket. Pelargoniums, petunias, lobelia, busy lizzie, nasturtiums. Only pelargoniums might lay claim to native ancestry, and many roses are far from English. This in a suburban garden in which nowadays you can sit and hear music from all over the world too, whether you want to or not but a great improvement on so-called 'Folk' music. Morris bells thankfully are intermittent and pub-related, and it is some time since my peace was invaded by a strolling minstrel.

I used to wish profoundly to live 'abroad', for years I yearned for hot climate, warm sea, exciting and interesting people, exotic music and interesting food. Since then everything has arrived on my doorstep as to my wishing, except the clean sea. Perhaps when the polar icecaps melt this will happen. I would now detest living in a very hot climate, even the south of France would be undesirable to me, because the type and variety of plants would be too limiting. In some parts of France you have to rush out and protect your plants from hot winds or they dry up immediately. I can grow passiflora here, and yucca, I could grow a grapevine here, I can grow many exotic things here, but in the south of France I could not grow a *Meconopsis cambrica*, or a *Geranium robertiana* 'Celtic White' (a tiny delightful thing which some might have thought of as a weed until it became rare), many ferns would be impossible and so on. The British Isles is ideal for gardening. The variety of plants which will thrive here is immense. With, of course, the correct care for some exotics. These procedures can be learned.

I even had to be told (long ago) that dahlias had to be dug up and stored indoors for the winter or the frost would kill them. As this also applies to potatoes, another South American plant, I should not have been so surprised, but I only discovered recently that fact about potatoes, never having grown them. It is the kind of information so taken for granted that when someone tells you that the common spud is an exotic, you just stare. Gosh I was surprised and interested – and even more so when I learned that dahlias too are a South American plant and go along with Aztecs, Incas, rhumba dance skirts and endless coffee. Well, last year I grew a wonderful dahlia with the rather typically British name of 'Grenadier', because it is a startlingly beautiful clear red with a gold centre and dark red stems. It reaches a metre tall and I grew it in a twenty-three centimetre dark blue glazed pot, quite successfully. In autumn I simply allowed the compost to dry out, cut the plant down and put the pot in the cellar until late spring. It is now flowering again, (July) twice as large as last year, and a bit cramped. Next autumn I shall unpot it, do the right thing by storing it in loose newspaper in the cellar, which never freezes, and the following spring cut it into suitable pieces as if for cooking a large artichoke, but with a sterile scalpel, and start all over again with more pots. Not conventional but anything can be tried at least once. I'd do anything for that dahlia. I really wanted a 'Bishop of Llandaff' but they can be hard to come by and 'Grenadier' popped into my line of sight at a nursery.

So we have no quarrel with the limitations of where we live geographically; the British climate is notorious as a subject of conversation but, nevertheless, it is still, the conservatory effect notwithstanding, inexcusable not to have a varied and fabulous garden. If your garden is not pleasing, it is the fault of the gardener. Only the size of my garden limits me. And this can be a virtue if you call it control rather than limitation. I have seen some dreadfully boring large gardens, beautifully situated large spreads of good earth largely given over to lawn and *déja vu* trees, gaudy umbrellas and seat-covers attracting all the visual attention left over from the shock of horrid modern roses stuck into crumbly beds of wasted soil. Their owners simply do not deserve generous gardens. Lost opportunity brings out unworthy emotions in me, rather like those felt when seeing another woman expensively dressed in perfectly awful taste. Jealousy, greed, envy and smugness in pride at the certain knowledge that one's own brilliant self looks a lot better in some worn old thing or a bit of cheap home sewing.

'What? Three hundred pounds? Crikey, I got *this* at Help the Aged for 50p.' Well, perhaps I'm not quite that bad, but I can't help a bit of let's call it sheer delight that in my one strip of earth nine metres by half a metre I currently have planted and thriving eighty-seven different plants. I mean, different varieties of plant. No garden is complete until not a centimetre of bare soil can be seen. If the plant collecting mania gets a hold of you, this may not take very long.

But how does it all begin?

2

How Not to Begin

There have been many disasters in my horticultural beginnings, but, if you do not count trying to start a market garden in a windswept overgrown patch at the far end of the terrace of a seventeenth century hall, when I knew utterly nothing about market gardening, I think the worst of all was the ghastly episode referred to by a few tasteless souls as a miniature Aberfan. This was a very long time before I even met MGF, and a couple of years before I had read Rachel Carson's classic book, Silent Spring, or it could not have happened.

I sinned totally against the environment, nature, the universe, and I was perfectly punished. I wasn't to know (that old excuse), but as it says in stone carved letters over the door of the police station at King Cross in Halifax: 'Ignorance of the Law Excuses No Man'. I've always thought that very unfair, really, but the uncarved postscript goes: 'Learn the Law and You'll be Okay'. I was stupid. Out of touch with things I valued.

I'd known I was a pantheist ever since studying Wordsworth at school, so how come at about age thirty could I have got so out of tune with Nature (whoever she is) that I thought a good way to start a garden was to poison the soil? One partial explanation is that a keynote of life at that time was the imported idea of 'labor-saving'. I had already noticed that using a twintub washer was hardly less labour-saving than scrubbing the clothes by hand, and that cleaning a badly designed electric cooker is as much trouble as cleaning the ashes from a kitchen range, but somehow thought and action do not always concur. And as for defrosting the fridge compared with wiping down the stone shelves in a pantry . . . Nevertheless labour-saving immediately sprang to mind in the matter of gardening, for we had moved into a modern house built on solid clay, with a very steep slope going straight up from the back onto an elevated lawn below a wood. The whole area was deeply overgrown, and I had three young children to feed from a rapidly iced-up fridge, and a twintub washer continually sloshing away. I could not face digging out all that couch grass and other tenacious herbiage, I had wrestled with the stuff before and lost. Excuses, excuses.

Now, I would cover the lot up for a season or so until it simply died from lack of light, but such simple methods did not exist in those days, in that place. I had previously done some pretty extensive slash-and-burn, using shears and something you never see now, a flame gun.

I'd had a lot of fun with that flame gun, it seemed the perfect answer to weeds, especially dandelions on the aforementioned terrace. In case you don't know, dandelions thrive on being burnt to the ground, they spring back redoubled in size and vigour overnight. The method was out for that and another reason. I had accidentally burned a frog which had been hiding under some leaves, which I had just time to see before it crawled out of reach under the old stone steps. I have rarely experienced such horror and remorse. The incident haunted me for a long time, causing me suddenly to shudder and put my face in my hands in the most unlikely places at unsuitable moments, and earning me part of my reputation as being somewhat barmy.

Before the flame gun was got rid of and after my horrors subsided and I looked for gentler methods of clearing the earth, I had another ghastly adventure. The lawn at the top of the steep jungle being overgrown I had the idea of getting it to a manageable state by burning it off quickly. The flames ran up the banking (like wildfire no less) and into the wood, a dense thicket about a mile deep, leading up to an abandoned mansion which I dreamed of owning. The wood was full of animals and birds, and was the adventure spot for several local children who trespassed happily there, judging by the hoots and laughter I sometimes heard. I had a vision of a forest fire even more frightening than the painting by Piero di Cosimo, The Forest Fire. Incidentally, MGF laughs at this painting at the same time as adoring it, because some of the fowl flying out of the wood on the right make him think of the chickens you see barbecued in takeaways, trying to escape.

I also had the most violent attack of panic I ever hope to experience. Adrenalin gave me the strength to run up and down those steep steps with buckets of water, screaming to the neighbour to get out her hosepipe (I hadn't got one at that time). That neighbour didn't like me and vice versa; to put it briefly she was a ghastly young snob, and to ask her for help with anything would have cost me too dear under normal circumstances. By the time she had rallied her brain sufficiently to fix the thing to a tap I had managed to put out the flames and fallen exhausted and shocked onto the back steps, trembling, hardly aware of her thinly veiled annoyance and joy that I had almost done something truly dangerous. The next day I bought some weedkiller.

I do not now recall which chemical it was, probably Agent Orange, but it would certainly have rendered barren a fair section of jungle. Very soon all the green disappeared completely, revealing an ugly, cracked building site. It was only then I began to regret the method, because a great many delightful plants had disappeared as well, and I particularly recalled wistfully the wild violets.

Then the rains came. Tropical downpours for days on end. I opened the back door one morning to find a slow-moving but relentless landslide of yellow mud already over the doorstep, completely filling the back path, which had brought down a section of retaining wall. Behind that was an area of steep mud the whole width of the property and about forty feet long, reaching to the height of the roof. Not a single root to hold it in place. I was peering up at a future dustbowl; the earth had replied to my insult!

It took us weeks, once the rainy season was over, to get all that completely rootless earth back where it belonged, bucket after bucket was hauled back up the bank, and meanwhile we could only use the front door. The neighbour was delighted. It dried out to loess enlivened with lumps of clay baked hard, and I had the task of cultivating it. In doing so I committed yet another ecological error which we had never heard of in those days of blithe ignorance. I incorporated approximately half of the Scottish moorland into that back patch. Every time I went out I exchanged yet more housekeeping money for a large bag of peat, and dug it in when I got home. This went on for months until finally the earth was ready to plant. Of course, now we know that peat simply evaporates when exposed to the air with digging, so all that destruction, money and effort would come to nothing in the end. Temporarily it lightened the soil with humus, and with that and grass cuttings and the occasional heap of leafmould dragged back from walks, plus a not very efficient compost heap I eventually created, it was possible to get things to grow. Clay is full of nutrients, but the plants cannot obtain them without organic matter present as well.

I was not, however, put off gardening, and eventually had some roses, vegetables, strawberries and a cherry tree growing out there, terraced below a creditable lawn. The first beetroot I pulled tasted horrible, bitter and burning, doubtless because it soaked up some residue of poison, but everything else was eventually okay, even some delicious carrots in a patch lightened with sand. The spinach and parsley were particularly successful, and the broad beans excellent. Everything grew on narrow terraces like a miniature version of those impossible slopes in the National Geographic. All I needed was a poncho and a bowler hat, so I could totter bravely along the little precipices with my primitive hoe. The weeds came back of course, so I had to dig them out after all. The violets did not return, and the thought of them even now makes me feel tearful and ashamed.

I have only once since then used weedkiller of any kind, on a gravel path, and even that was a worry in case a cat walked on it before it was dry. Having weeds is preferable to having poison, and digging out weeds is good exercise, done methodically and slowly.

Also of course, there is the matter of mulching. I had no idea what mulching was and hadn't the gumption to find out by reading. It is a word to conjure with, m-u-l-c-h-i-n-g. To mulch with relish. Deliciously mulchy. Dry Mulch (a little town in a cowboy movie). Mulching over a question. Mulchy Bar (real milk chocolate). Mulched: the state of your best skirt after a baby has vomited on it. Crossing the Mulch (a dangerous straits off the Isle of Arran, not navigable in winter). Mulchberry, a low-growing fruit of the Lapp tundra, staple food of prehistoric elks. Any or all of these I might have countenanced, but 'to put straw or other organic matter around the base of plants to keep in moisture and prevent growth of weeds', never. Too ridiculous for words. Who would do such a thing? Every gardener with a little knowledge, of course. Now a mulch can be plastic, old carpet, newspaper, anything which serves the purpose if you don't mind its appearance. I have yet to try coco shell to see if it deters slugs but have got around to bark chippings at last. Come to think of it, I could use up some old typescripts for mulching, perhaps they would keep slugs and snails busy reading the novels I wrote which have excited no human publisher. I think it slightly possible that lower life-forms may be able to read.

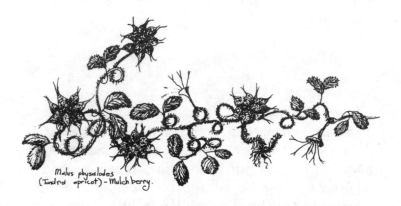

Malus physaloides
(Tundra apricot) - Mulch berry.

If I may digress a little further I would like to impart an excellent method of deterring ants from entering the house. I had been told by a wise old person (I forget who exactly) that if you did not want insects or other pests, all you had to do was speak seriously to them and ask them to leave. Wasps respond favourably to this approach so I tried this with the ants with some success but they kept returning, so I wrote a notice and pinned it to the skirting board in the downstairs bathroom. 'No ants allowed in this disco except in evening dress.' I never saw another one after that. I shall try something similar with my mollusc marauders just as soon as I've finished this chapter, and report back later in the book.

How not to begin!

But, how to begin a garden, with the least promising location imaginable, short of three square
yards in a Tibetan icefield, which can doubtless be
achieved during a thaw. I found myself here, in this
'town cottage', having left behind a large garden
which was coming along nicely, with no garden at all.
The previous owners had used the back yard for
heaping junk, mending motor bikes and not much
else. Most of the beautiful 'blue' brick sets had been
very roughly concreted over, the old brick walls
daubed with patches of the hideous bright blue paint
with which most of the house, inside and out, had
been thickly painted (perhaps to keep away the Evil
Eye, it can't have been from aesthetic choice,
surely?). The narrow strips of earth were a dry empty
dust (perhaps they had used weedkiller?) and there
was quite a lot of oldish catshit and a patch of tired
mint. Nothing else.

I remember the period between having made a
commitment to buy the property and actually
signing and moving, when I walked along the back
alley one sunny day and peered through a hole in the
high back gate. There was nothing to see but ugliness
and neglect, a mean space, and my spirits fell hard.
Where I still lived I had old apple trees supporting
vigorous species roses, a lush lawn, blackcurrant and
gooseberry bushes, lots of cosmos, nicotiana, a plum
tree weighed low the previous year with fabulous
yellow plums, various bulbs getting their feet in and
spreading and many other delights including annuals
which had thrived from seed and which I loved.
There was even room for some enormous teazles,
taller than myself, with hollows between stem and

leaf which filled with rainwater, a phenomenon I had never seen in such splendour. A clump of golden rod came up out of a crack every year, also taller than myself. How could I have even considered living in this ghastly little dump, what had I allowed to happen?

And then I had a vision, peering guiltily through that hole. I saw lovely pots full of thriving flowering plants, clematis climbing over the roof of the out-house, ivy covering the blue daubs, flourishing hanging baskets, herbs, lots of flowers. I saw a small but lush town garden with a bench and a small table, just sufficient space for a folding sunbed in the corner which was not overlooked. A little suntrap with style and grace and no greedy and thirsty lawn to trouble over, a haven for unusual plants, large flowers protected from harsh wind. I began to breathe again and crept away with my vision firmly placed in my mind.

Six years later an improved version of it has come into being. Perhaps a better gardener than I have been could have accomplished all this much sooner; I myself could with luck do better now. But this is the story of how this Garden Down a Rabbit Hole came into being. My impossible challenge, and its eventual success. So how to begin? I thought I knew already how not to begin, but I had never had such a small space before.

3

How It Began

Between leaving one garden (home) and moving into
the present house, there was an interval of three
months when I had to store all my furniture and be a
lodger. This was because the house required a lot of
work to make it at all habitable. French doors
replaced a window and a window replaced the
kitchen door, acres of ghastly tiles had to be
hammered off, ceilings stripped of insulating poly-
styrene tiles, and every wall surface got down to the
plaster. Miles of plastic wallpaper were removed,
layer upon layer of horrible stinking carpet taken up,
and then the plastic tiles beneath that, and then a
sanding machine employed to reveal good pine
boards. Broken bathroom fittings were removed,
along with great nests of pipes all knotted up in a
sinister serpentine manner wherever they would be
most visible. I became a regular at the town dump,
taking infinite carloads of junk and hurling it
joyfully towards the grabbers. Doors were stripped,
aluminium handles removed, wherever possible anything badly designed or out of tune with the original
Victorian house was jettisoned. Much original
beauty appeared, including a fossil marble fireplace
and a room with some original plasterwork
mouldings.

But more urgent than any of this to me was the

future of the garden. I had several plants in tubs and pots about which I was very anxious. There was a *Clematis* 'Henryi' doing quite nicely in a wooden tub much too heavy to lift, even with the statutory two strong men who fortunately appear at such times. I dug up the plant, disturbing its roots as little as possible, which was quite a lot and would have killed most clematis, put the whole thing along with its climbing frame, flat in the back of a borrowed estate car and within the hour had it planted opposite where the kitchen window would soon be, if only the builder would come back and continue the work. Builders never begin a thing and see it through, they juggle several jobs and their summer holidays all at once, meanwhile taking away with them large sums on account.

I drilled in the vine-eyes and tied up the 'Henryi' with love and good wishes, watered it, and felt a lot better. Such exploits incur anxiety sessions, until complete. The tub stood empty in another part of the yard, someday to be filled with something wonderful. But the clematis had found a home.

'Henryi' is a lovely variety with large simple white flowers, needs no pruning and will grow in a shady place, or so MGF told me, which was why I chose it in the first place. I could see it covering that rather horrible patch of spoiled brick wall the next spring. To make quite sure the wall would get covered I transplated a chunk of 'Goldheart' ivy from a corner of my former garden and got that tucked in straight away. I also managed to transplant some ginger mint, a grey ivy which looks like Gorgonzola cheese, some eau-de-Cologne mint and some white daffodils

which I cherished. The garden had begun. I did
nothing to the soil, just pushed the plants in with my
usual words of *bonne chance*. When I moved in at the
beginning of the autumn, with some of the rooms
decorated and a livable house begun, MGF visited.

'That "Henryi" will die, it isn't planted deeply
enough,' he mournfully pronounced. There is a
certain subtle tone in MGF's 'mournful' voice which
more accurately could be described as glee, but I try
not to hear it, like one of the three wise monkeys.
'Henryi' die! No! There was no way to replant it then
because it had twined itself around my wires strung
to vine-eyes, I just could not see how such a job could
be done. It had apparently survived one impossible
relocation, over and above taking it from its nursery
pot into its tub, but another upheaval, in only a few
weeks? I thought not. I was wilting from my own
transplanting, and knew how it would feel. If I
missed my huge Victorian sitting-room with its large
open fire and abundant light, how would 'Henryi'
feel, all clematis notoriously disliking home re-
movals. But his words, delivered like a judge to an
innocent prisoner, were a challenge I could not turn
from.

'It will live, it will love it there, it will be okay,
you'll see,' I told him. When he had gone I gently dug
in some fresh compost, covered its roots with peat,
(we still hadn't learned about peat), stood a small
trough across its roots supported on two bricks, to
shelter them from midday sun, and turned to yet
more indoor pursuits as winter approached.

There were several indoor plants to accommodate,
including a fifteen-foot kangaroo vine which I

31

wanted to cover the dining-room wall opposite the new french doors. The amount of light in the room was less than I had anticipated, because I had refused modern slender-framed doors as being unsuitable and got harmonious wooden frames. The walls were painted white, mirrors were introduced, but it was still too gloomy for a native of Australia. I got some special lightbulbs at high cost, and constructed a special shade to direct the life-saving light onto the plant, but still it did not thrive as it had before. Leaves dropped continually. I moved it into the bathroom and gladly rearranged the dining-room so that it could be used by people. After a two-year struggle I lost the vine. I had owned it for ten years, but that too had spent three months on someone else's landing, temporarily strung up towards a skylight, and had possibly sulked itself to death. Meanwhile 'Henryi' thrived wonderfully.

The following spring it bore several huge perfect flowers on the growth it had managed before the cold weather set in. I had planted some yellow corydalis, donated grandly by MGF, to help fill in the few inches of soil in the bed, and that thrived also, making a fern-like mound around the small trough. The 'Goldheart' ivy climbed rapidly and had soon poked itself across onto the new garden door, getting its fingers greedily in under and around the new wood in a delightful Pre-Raphaelite manner, promising to cover a horrible old fall pipe which should have been removed but had got overlooked in the general upheaval. Daffodils emerged but refused to flower. A male fern took happily to the foot of the ivy, uncoiling quickly as the weather improved. What else could I plant there? Some London pride? As I began to probe with my trowel, I hit something with a clang. Buried treasure? No. Solid concrete, or stone; ah yes, both.

The whole of that corner had just a skimming of earth on it, and triumphant 'Henyri' had been planted right at the edge of it, only just in proper soil. I was devastated, of course. No flowers there, nothing with long roots. The ivy and the fern grow very well in it, but obviously nothing else would. It was too dark for alpines and in any case I had not ventured into that area of horticulture yet. It was some time before I hit upon the solution.

I bought a couple of chimney pots, different heights, from a builder's merchant, and put ferns in them, tucking the London pride in around their bases. I had also bought a sick-looking mystery plant at a garden-centre sale, with spotted leaves and the information that it was a climber. I daringly transplanted it from another place where it was already overgrown with the nasty mint, having imagined it climbing up the wall. It was put into one chimney pot along with a fern. I was still confused about how plants climb, some needing something to twine around and some having their own suckers, but if this was a climber, then it would climb, wouldn't it? A potentially barren corner looked like proper garden. Any other containers might have done as well and been cheaper, but I had been in a panic and wanted something which looked good from the kitchen window. I later squeezed in a plastic epergne under the male fern, containing a fern of its own, and the container itself has become invisible. It would be some long time before the brick wall would be anything like disguised, but to my hopeful eyes the process was well under way. I proudly displayed my initial efforts to MGF.

'Oh, that's not a climber it's a shrub. You've got an *Abutilon megapotamicum* "Variegata" there I think, and it will die. For only one thing, it isn't fully hardy.'

'Well neither am I and I'm still alive,' I snapped back, secretly drawing nearer to my end but bravely saying nothing. I left the perhaps climbing abutilon where it was. Perhaps a miracle would occur? All gardening is something of a miracle, after all.

In that rather dank couple of metres where the soil became deeper, I planted tiger lilies, some leucojums and (don't laugh) some gentians. How did I know that gentians hate limey soil? How could anyone know? Well, I soon got to know because MGF told me, but this was just as they were, very quickly, on their last breath poor things. You know about gentians because I've just told you, if you are not one of those gardeners like MGF who know everything. Never, but never try gentians, in anything but acid soil. Some are said to thrive in neutral or even slightly limey soil, but almost all of them prefer not to have to struggle so hard. I loved that brilliant blue flower, just the one, and it was to be years before I dared try them again.

Two years before moving I had been given a present of two azaleas and had brought them with me from the former garden, where I had in fact made what I fondly believed to be an acid bed for them (I did know a bit you see), where they had done moderately well. One was the orange one which I eventually gave away, and another was a ground-cover type with magenta flowers. In they went, not far from the foot of the clematis, notorious for its hatred of acid. I was dismayed when the azaleas got yellowing leaves, and consulted MGF on the matter. He laughed with a peculiarly scornful laugh reserved for ignorant gardeners, a laugh which I have come to detest and dread, because it means humiliation, doom, disgrace. Useless for me to point out that I had dressed the soil with peat, that simply was not enough.

I transferred the orange azalea into a plastic tub which I stood on top of the soil, filled with coir which is neutral, but the other one would just have to fight, for there was no ground for a ground cover plant to cover. I should not have been so possessive, and left it back in the bed I had made for it. After all, I had suffered enough making that acid bed.

I had dug out two feet of soil at the foot of a fence, about six feet by six at least, lined it with black polythene at the back to cover the cement in which the fenceposts were set, and tipped in lots of expensive and non-ecological peat. Peat soaks up lots of water, which is much of its point, so I had the hosepipe going as I dug it in and thickly scattered it on the bed, turning it over and over to be thoroughly wetted. Of course, the local water is very limey so I was defeating my purpose even as I worked, but my brain, thickly stuffed as it is with lots of useless but fascinating scientific knowledge, had not reminded me of that. I recall school chemistry lessons where I learned that an alkali and an acid mixed produces carbon dioxide, I knew that dock leaves (acid) soothe wasp stings (alkali) or should that be bee stings? – well, I *was* the only person in the class who knew what a catalyst is, indeed I am a catalyst. It's a wonder the garden didn't explode like champagne or swell up like a baking-powder cake. Did I pause to reflect that Leamington water, notorious for its alkaline qualities as well as its filthy taste would not be good for azaleas? No. Again, I was punished for my idiocy. Almost fatally this time, a case of Instant Karma.

I finally decided that the peat was all moistened and that it was time to plant my azaleas, my heathers, and my cytisus. I had enjoyed all that work in the fresh air, I felt good, I had been daydreaming. And I was stuck. I had sunk over my welly-tops into a peat bog, slowly but surely sucked, planted myself rather tastefully against a fence, the evening sun about to catch my brave smile as I disappeared. I have always had a terror of bogs. I once had to wobble across a large deep one in the Peak District when I went on a lone camping trip, and it took me about a half hour to get up my courage, having had a vision of my twenty-five kilo back-pack pressing me into an early grave, to be preserved for a thousand years until some future archeologist should find Camping Woman, mosquito bites still intact. This adventure was muckier but quicker, I somehow managed to spring out of my wellies and skim rapidly back to the lawn where I was found on my back having hysterics, pointing speechlessly at my wellies which had gone. I think they are still there.

Gardening can be terrific fun. I should have left that azalea to mark my almost-grave. It eventually died a protracted death, from a cause which I will reveal later.

Meanwhile, I had adapted, not only to smaller rooms, which I had not lived in for about twenty years, but to the all-consuming idea of making this back patch a Garden of Eden rather than merely a respectable area. Not that many people kowtow excessively towards back yards here in Leamington, for so many of the elegant Regency and Victorian mansions have mature spreads complete with statuary, lawn, conservatory, pond and even barbecue, the last idea being borrowed from the council estates who were into them immediately Neighbours was screened. But I wanted something more than mere tidiness. I wanted Art, Atmosphere, Attitude. I planted a Virginia creeper, and some jasmine.

Oh, God, that jasmine. I had seen it growing for

the first time here in Leamington, in a sheltered garden up a very high wall, its beautiful leaves making unmistakable Chinese watercolour patterns and shadows. I coveted some. Its owner warned me of its vigour, but this only made me desire it more. Jasmine! The scent, the delightful leaves, the fact that it was evergreen, obviously perfect for disguising the place where the bricks had been changed about with my alterations. I was given some young shoots and these I planted in the small planter built by the back doorstep. I gave it some wires to climb up by a very complicated and interesting method, without a ladder, by swinging weighted wires across from one window to another, having drawn them up by a length of knitting wool suspended, nailing them to the barge boards at the top by standing on a chair and leaning out of the top light with a hammer, and vine-eyes at the bottom.

It was in this planter that a Virginia creeper was also put, because I'd seen a magnificent example of it on the huge wall of an undertaker's not far away. The fabulous sheet of flaming colour had captivated me.

MGF warned me very seriously about both of these plants. He said that not only were they rather common (in Leamington, but not anywhere else I had lived and certainly not in Halifax) but they really were too vigorous, and would rapidly become a nuisance. I could not listen to such stuff. However, in under two years they were both up onto the roof, across the windows, around the gutters and under the tiles, not to mention forming a dense bush just out of reach so that no light could penetrate the dining-room or the bedroom above. There was a lot of jasmine scent, for just one season, and then thousands of jasmine flowers and sheaves of scarlet leaves. The jasmine has overcome even the Virginia creeper now, it pokes out here and there morosely, defiantly dropping a few red leaves as if weeping blood. Yes, both plants are a nuisance. I had a passing builder (doubtless having left somebody with a wall half built) control it seriously for me but this only seemed to encourage it, except into flowering profusely again. It also oozes a strangely unshiftable resin onto window-glass, I do not suppose they will ever be clear again. I began, eventually, to hate it. I am currently in the process of cutting it off partway up the stems so the top stuff will die off sufficiently for it to be cut and shoved into not too many compost sacks, probably about a dozen I guess. I shall have to pay someone to bring a ladder and do this job. I will suffer much for my garden, but not vertigo beyond a stepladder. Do not plant jasmine or Virginia creeper unless you want to play at Lost Temples in the Yucatan (or Lost Causes). The same advice pertains with species roses, of course. I suspect that the owner of my former garden is currently asleep for a hundred years, exhausted from trying to get out to the dustbin. All these and many other lovely creepers and twiners are for truly enormous gardens.

Before winter comes, that corner must be cleared. I tremble to think of the hard work I will have digging out its roots. I may have to use a poison such as brushwood killer, but I certainly hope not. I apologise to the jasmine as I cut it. But with survival tactics like that, I don't think it is in as much danger of extinction as I am. If I don't kill it, the thing will eat me.

My advice on how to begin is advice on how not to begin, because this is how gardening happens. There are actually lots of books on how to begin, but all their excellent plans cost about a thousand pounds and involve new topsoil, expensive compost, landscaping with expensive stones, statues, fountains, ponds, and involve either your whole existence or the aid of electricians and the elusive builder, even before you go near a nursery with a carefully thought out list of plants.

Gardening on the cheap is still expensive, but you don't need a second mortgage. And all the pleasure as well as the pain is your own. What is usually needed are improved soil, light, and air, this last preferably not at gale force. Therefore I began quite wrongly by introducing shade (from the jasmine for example) over a place where I wanted brilliant sunny colour. It is from this and other mistakes that I learned a lot about gardening in the shade, of course, so all was not lost. Margery Fish's wonderful book on the subject illuminated a lot of my darkness, but I had to try things for myself, and so will you, because every plant in its location is a unique experiment. As with painting, there are no formulae, gardening by numbers can never add up. Would you have grown jasmine, given the opportunity, before you read my words of warning? Confess. You would. It is beautiful stuff – in China tea. And perhaps you still will grow it, and all shall be well. I gave some roots to a person whose mother wanted to cover an unsightly garage, who could not imagine its vigour. I bet she can't get the car out now.

So I began to learn, and am still doing so, both from MGF and from my own mistakes. But for the first two years my initial plantings seemed very hopeful and promise-filled. Some of my ideas were good ones, and so were some of his. MGF is not always as sensible as he might be. I have to say this.

We discussed various climbers, shrubs, things to put in a tub; I planted some things behind his back and he sneaked in a few behind mine.

I planted a pale pink climbing rose ('Ice Maiden'), which I thought would be scented and was not, although it has some virtues. And a ribes because they were one of the first shrubs I loved as a child. He sneered at the ribes (every council house has one of those things, darling, whatever are you thinking of, and it will get too big as well for where you've planted it, you won't be able to get past it once it gets going blah blah) – *and* I planted a *Clematis montana.* I planted a Japanese honeysuckle.

He planted ordinary honeysuckle, just a couple of little sticks stuck in the earth which I knew would die. They didn't, I have been obliged to cut out and untangle hundreds of yards of it, but the flowers are so beautiful and so heavily scented in a good year that it is more than worth the trouble. He planted *Iris foetidissima* and hostas over which he goes somewhat crazy. He insisted I have a *Parthenocissus henryana.*

This climber has very beautiful leaves, and is, as he told me at some length, vastly superior in every way to Virginia creeper. But once it gets its feet in, it too is extremely vigorous and needs a lot of pruning, so beware. It does cover a wall behind other plants, though, and fights for supremacy over the *montana*. To date they are about equal.

And in the tub, after he had caused me by a particularly coruscating bout of sneering to remove an *ordinary* buddleia, he insisted that I plant his gift of a very young *Rhus typhina*. This was unfortunately a male specimen, thus not giving red flowers, but it is very beautiful and I was delighted to have it. He does have trouble sexing creatures sometimes; one year his male budgerigar laid eggs. And come to think of it, *Rhus typhina* is just about everywhere, once you know what to look for. It is the where and the way it is grown which makes all the difference and, apart from this one not having the red flowers, it was wonderful for a few years, like a miniature palm-tree, very graceful. Its single stem leaned over to one side and then gave a balancing stem at the top, giving the impression of a bonsai.

Everyone admired this small tree, but nobody noticed the clump of *Iris feotidissima* at its base, partly because of the increasing shade as the large fans of rhus leaves increased, and partly because this particular iris is not spectacular. It is not common however, and when the flowers finally appear, in early spring, they are extremely complex and subtly coloured, and well worth long close examination. They are so named because they are said to smell of rotten meat, especially when moved, but I have never noticed even a hint of this in mine. They produce huge green seedpods which eventually open to reveal wonderful red berries, perfectly globular and shining, which will stay on the plant all through winter and into next spring, and add another bit of winter colour which is, of course, very important. I split this clump eventually when it got too large and the other half has taken very well in another shady spot where I can see its berries in winter from the kitchen window, after two years waiting until it felt at home. I have twice found some growing wild in Wales and in the Isle of Skye, and seen them once in someone else's garden, so for these somewhat rare irises I thank MGF very much.

Another lovely thing for which I thank him is also a part of this tub in recent years. He first made me buy some for the previous garden but of course they got left behind. They are snake's-head fritillaries, or *Fritillaria meleagris*, a delicate hanging bell about an inch in diameter, and in the purple ones especially the most remarkable markings I have ever seen in a flower. They are actually chequered, which perhaps makes them look somewhat like snakeskin. These bells depend from extremely slender stalks with slim leaves. I also have some white ones (*pallidiflora*), which are even better in a shady spot against other dark green leaves. They used to grow wild in the British Isles, in watery meadows, but are now very rare in any numbers. There are still two exemplary meadows full of them which I know of, one in Oxford and one not far from Cheltenham, and the bulbs are protected. Those you buy are not purloined from the wild but bred, and as far as I can tell identical with the species. I wouldn't be without them now, they flower quite early and go on until the end of May sometimes. They swing about in the strongest wind without breaking and the flowers last a long time. No garden is complete without at least one group of these flowers, and here I quote MGF who is often perfectly right.

I really do not know if alone I would have discovered and cultivated many of the plants to which he has introduced me, but I certainly hope so. The credit must go to him for several discoveries and, of course, how this was done was by his recommending lots of books to look at and read, his thrusting seed and bulb catalogues at me, and best of all, taking me to other gardens to show me plants. Lots of these expeditions were before our long phase of garden exploration during my convalescence, but long before that he had been talking horticulture to me and educating me even before I knew it. He it was who introduced me to Himalayan balsam, for the garden before my very large one. Beautiful pink orchid-like flowers on tall stems, to fill in spaces until I got a pile of builder's rubble transformed into a lawn. Never have I hated a plant so much. From a couple of tiny seedlings it shot up and seeded literally millions of others in what seemed like six weeks but must presumably have been a year. For months I seemed to do nothing except scrape out Himalayan balsam seedlings from every possible crumb of earth. Those that survived to adulthood had thick juicy stems which broke at a touch, spurting out disgusting foaming sap in a sinister manner reminiscent of the Triffids. There is some of this plant at the wonderful Mill Street Garden in Warwick, not far from the remarkable gunnera. Next time I visit I must ask how he manages to keep it under control. In my opinion the Himalayas is just about the right sized patch for that kind of balsam, and it might conceivably be classed with hogweed as a dangerous pest. But that plant is only one of several hundred which MGF dotes upon, not all so obtrusive, and it is many years now since he began to infect me with his enthusiasm, and wanted to show me various successful plantings.

Visiting gardens, with or without the knowledge of their owners, with MGF, has been a series of rich experiences for me.

4

Out and About with MGF

MGF gardens professionally for chosen people, when he is in the mood, and it just so happened that when I moved in here, he was helping a friend of his with a similar patch further down the street. I had previously met this person, and knew he lived nearby, but was not on neighbouring terms. It transpires that they (he has since then become a 'partner' and a father) are what might be described as exclusive people in any case, and I am on neighbouring terms with nobody; popping in and out of houses and tolerating poppers is not for me. MGF described the garden he was creating for them, two people who knew nothing at all about gardening, and he was enthusiastic about what could be achieved in a limited space.

The garden was not so limited as mine, however, because mine has an early extension built onto it, in the same style and old Leamington brick, and although the house is two metres wider than any other on the street, and was probably the builder's own house, it has therefore much less garden area. According to MGF, his patrons not only knew nothing whatsoever about gardening, but cared about as much and just wanted it to look nice. This is not, of course, enough for MGF, who was really going to town on making it unusual and interesting and marvellous. He described his invention of a garden seat built against a wall, slatted, and meant to be lifted up when not in use, the opposite of a loo seat, so that light could penetrate to the low-growing plants underneath. He also told me that he was cultivating an *Actinidia chinensis*, which is a kiwi fruit, along a north-facing wall, on invisibly placed green wires. There was a small lawn and lots of interesting plants coming along nicely. MGF told me all this over coffee one teabreak when he had called during one of my bouts of garden despair. MGF is one of the few people allowed to 'pop' in.

'Come along and see it, why not, I've got a key,' he said. I was borne along the street on his wave of enthusiasm, and we went in through the front door, to my surprise, for I had thought he meant the key to the garden door. We went straight through to the garden, I feeling most uneasy, and he began to show me all the progress he had made. It was certainly very promising, and I was just at the stage of thinking that I could never, ever, get mine to look anything like as good, when out came the owner of the house, with the crossest and most suspicious look on his face I ever hope to see. He said nothing, but it was clear that I easily fulfilled the role of intruder, and that MGF too was in disfavour. It was deeply embarrassing, and after a few minutes of polite talk about the garden, we left in silence. MGF just shrugged, this kind of thing is not his concern. It took me years to dissolve the memory, and only recently has it gone sufficiently far into the past for me to manage a bit of relaxed chat with this person if I see him on the street. I am cautious ever since about where I do in fact go to look at plants with my friend. His code is not quite the same as mine.

Years later, that man is leaving for a larger house with a more generous garden, and MGF will again be employed there in the autumn. I shall require an invitation from its owner, which I shall be surprised to receive, before going anywhere near. I shall rely on MGF's detailed reports.

Even having seen an actinidia beginning to thrive, I had no faith that I could achieve the same result. I simply felt that it would be too exotic, especially against a north-facing wall, and refused point blank to have one. I was told that after he stopped doing that garden it deteriorated, largely due to their cat which scratched things up and poisoned them, and also from sheer neglect. If MGF did not do the upkeep, which is rather beneath his extraordinary talents, things went downhill. MGF is a dedicated cat-lover, but this particular cat he began to hate viciously, because of its deadly tomcat aim at the roots of anything he planted. At the time I hardly registered what he was saying with regard to cats and gardens. Eventually actinidia had come away from the wall, weighted down with snow as I recall, and was in a heap, and MGF was almost in tears.

Then a friend of mine who was buying a very large house and garden, the back of which abutted onto my street, asked me if I knew anyone who could renovate her garden for her. She was having a lot of building and other alterations done to make the top floors into flats, part of the downstairs into con- sulting rooms, an outside staircase descending from a balcony at the back, and so on, all in splendid taste.

'Well yes I think I do, if he is available,' I replied. 'MGF is your best possible person because he knows about the right sort of aura a garden like this should have.' She wanted everything 'in keeping' with the early Victorian mansion, but knew only a little of the subject and had no time at all to spare. It was all rampantly overgrown, but filled with promise. I was deeply envious, as what potentially obsessed gardener would not be. I had got my jasmine from this person from her former house, and recalled her saying something about its excessive capacity for growth, which I had not noted at the time. This garden had room for jasmine. It had room for a wistaria, a grapevine, a pond, a vegetable garden. It had a pear tree and dozens of shrubs. She knew MGF slightly, but he had not immediately sprung to mind, so she asked me to find him and ask him to call and discuss the matter, if he was at all interested.

Months were to pass before I got these two together. The woman is busy, travels a lot, and MGF is wonderful at procrastination. The future receives his most intense attention. To be fair, of course, gardening does require a lot of planning.

But when he finally called at her house, at a time to suit his somewhat unconventional schedule, she was so glad to see him at all that they got along extremely well. Ideas and inspirations occurred and were tossed around joyfully, plans were drawn, and actual work soon began. Thus it was that when he had been working in her garden, he would often end the day by leaving via the back gate and coming over to visit me. I began to know her garden by report in great detail. Sometimes we would go along to a pub either before or after a meal, and the talk was almost all about gardening. I had a blow by blow account of the progress being made. And then I was invited by the garden owner herself to come across and see the progress, a much more satisfactory way to view a garden. We had tea, and then the tour. There was plenty to see, even if it was not yet there. The reality which MGF can conjure just by speaking and pointing is much superior to anything on the lower plane upon which most of us dwell.

The area is probably about thirty metres in length and twenty-three metres across, possibly more. It has three metre high brick walls all down either side and a much higher wall with a gate in one corner which leads to my street. My front bedroom window can just be seen from her back balcony. A path goes around to the front, with flower beds either side, and these alone constitute more earth than I own altogether. MGF was to have his work cut out.

Now, I have indicated that MGF is something of a visionary, or as some mean souls would have it an impractical daydreamer, but my other friend, whom I shall now refer to by her first initial of S, is even more so. Not only that, she knows her own mind, and is extremely obstinate in some things and hates to be crossed. These two circled one another like Kung Fu fighters for supremacy of ideas on plants and where they should be grown. I was cast in the role of mediator, the objective voice and sympathetic ear whenever either one of them could catch me without the other present. I learned a great deal about horticulture and human nature over the few years during which the garden progressed, sometimes by leaps and bounds but mostly by fits and starts. MGF was constantly on the point of 'letting her get on with it herself if she knows so much, let her ruin it all, all my work wasted . . .' and more in that vein, and S would telephone me to ask for her gardener's whereabouts, for she had not seen him for more than a week and things were getting on top of her, the things in the pots were wilting, what should she do? I would advise her to water them whilst I went in search of MGF, who does not like the telephone and has to be called upon, a great nuisance to everyone who wishes to see him. I had the instructive task of weighing the pros and cons of their points of view.

The biggest contention was about roses.

There were already several long-established roses there, but, oh horrors, they were modern roses. You only have to say 'modern roses' to MGF and he throws his hands in the air and lets out a long series of groans and sneers enough to kill one should it be listening. One of S's which he particularly had it in for had large orange blooms, and only one of its offensive habits was that not only was it in the wrong place, according to his plan, it was shouting obscenities into his colour scheme. It was too strong for him and his curses, it thrived. And S adored the thing. I could see what he meant. The rose had little to be said for it aesthetically, but it was astonishly healthy, no aphid would touch it and blackspot bypassed it as unsuitable. When I first saw it and others of similar ilk in glorious Dayglo colours, they were overgrown with various weeds and long dry grass, but thriving away, looking like handsful of crumpled dinner napkins thrown from a children's party. They are the sort of roses which deface our parks, which we are forced to pay money for and walk past if we want a breath of air when in town. They stick there in bare earth, triumphantly gaudy and meaningless, usually with no scent. Yes, I could see what he meant. He wanted to root them all out and replace them with old garden varieties, most of which of course have much shorter periods of flowering, but how marvellous they really are.

But S too had a point, which was that the roses, even when the garden was overgrown, had given her such heavenly pleasure especially when she went outdoors to meditate shortly after dawn (this is all true by the way) and that to murder them would be a crime. My point was that perhaps MGF could be allowed to rearrange them, modify their blatancy somewhat, and that after all, it was *her* garden and not his. The battle went on and I began to suspect that in some grim way they were enjoying it.

I began to be exasperated with him myself when he spoke of this garden, because he had such grandiose plans for it I did not see how they could possibly be effected. The garden was large, but not that large.

A patio appeared outside her consulting room french windows, originally intended by MGF to be of gravel in an especially delicate colour and size which I could not see the point of but I said nothing, with a smart half-circle of old bricks carefully demarcating where it joined the lawn. It had turned out to be of ordinary gravel because of the enormous cost of obtaining the special stuff, and it looked just fine. In the centre of the lawn was a circular area done in the same way, about a metre across, where S wanted some kind of object with mystical significance around which to walk while meditating. We had hilarious times speculating upon what this might be. She wanted some kind of seated Buddha or a Kali but I thought this was rather too Disneyland on this scale; Cupid and wild boars were of course completely out, as was a small fountain with some grossly indecent source of water. He had persuaded her to buy a particularly lovely slab of very old hard stone, and it was suggested that this might be stood up like some ancient menhir, but the mechanics were too tricky as it could have fallen onto her if not a third buried, which would hide too much of it. This now lies in the gravel looking lovely when it trips people up. S has always been something of a feminist in a religious way (goddess), which I am not against of course, but my naughtier side suggested an enormous phallus might look quite fetching (she likes men) but possibly too distracting at meditation time. A pyramid was a possibility, or a horned moon reminiscent of Knossos. A sundial was my favourite but considered too tame by both of them, and a stone

globe on a pillar was the final decision. It has not yet materialised, and some thrifts and pinks look very nice there, enlivened by eschscholzia.

MGF wanted to plant a nut grove in between the vegetable patch and the 'wild garden' behind the border around the lawn. Much of this would be shaded by an enormous old pear tree, and I thought there was a slim chance of it becoming anything but part of the wilderness area. I maintain strongly that there is actually no such thing as a wild garden. Gardens are human artefacts, carefully controlled, possibly to look very natural, but wild, never. If you leave all the gardening to nature, god or goddess, it tends to get merely overgrown in a single season. So we argued about that quite a lot, but the nut grove was to be called the Shrine Walk, and at the end of it, in a secret place, was to be something very special. What this might eventually be was never decided. I thought a small fountain and a lot of ferns would be lovely but this too was tame. The actual hazels are thriving now, so all is not lost.

Another must was a pond complete with small Chinese style bridge across it. There simply was not sufficient space, anyone could see that, but they both thought it a lovely idea and went out to look at pond liners. It transpired that all the plumbing and building for that as well as a small fountain on the patio would be too expensive for a while, so as yet that too is in the land of dreams. But it was an exciting phase, this planning and beginning, and MGF worked hard, not only to persuade S to his way of thinking, but to effect some major improvements. Part of the trouble with his sense of scale is, I think, that he has culled a lot of his ideas and love of gardens from the large stately homes of England. To anyone with less imagination and more practicality it is obvious that what can be achieved at Hidcote and Kiftsgate cannot be done in even a large back garden in town. MGF said that I needed to be shown what gardening really was, so our days out began in earnest. I received revelations. I was changed by these visits.

It began with Hidcote, in the nearby Cotswolds, one blazing summer day shortly after I had got myself mobile again, and was fit to drive. We took a picnic and set off in the morning full of expectancy. MGF was very excited, for not only had he not been to Hidcote for a while, he knew that it was going to change me. He had taken on the role of guru, and was waiting to watch my face as I looked around in wonder. He was not disappointed.

Hidcote was presented to the National Trust in 1948 by its owner and creator, Lawrence Johnston, an American born in France and educated in England. He came to Hidcote in 1907 at the age of thirty-five, and began his creating of gardens. Here is gardening on a scale and with vision beyond the scope of ordinary mortals. I had certainly never seen anything as wonderful outside of Kew or the Botanical Gardens in Edinburgh, and neither of these has quite the note of both grandeur and intimacy to be experienced at Hidcote. I was already struck with awe by the time we had entered what is known as the Garden Yard.

Over some lovely old sheds, the style of which took me back to my childhood, grows a marvellous wistaria, twisted, gnarled and floriferous, a thing of wonder. Arthur Rackham fairies live in wistarias like this, and I think I saw one but you can never be sure. I was distracted by a beautiful old lead cistern in which grew the most successful and delicious creamy fuchsia I had ever seen, or, to be more exact, had noticed in such detail. When MGF takes you to a garden, you are not allowed to walk by anything beautiful and interesting remarking 'how pretty'; you look, and listen. Remembering everything is a different matter of course, but I do know that this fuchsia was not hardy and therefore, having no greenhouse I could not have that particular one, it was far too large for any windowsill of mine.

'Oh, there are thousands of hardy fuchsias you can have, come along!' he ordered, and we entered the Theatre Lawn. Hidcote is a garden of contrasts, divided into 'rooms' each one quite different from the last. There is a large stage at the far end, and the whole lawn is enclosed by immaculate tall hedges. On the stage stands an enormous beech, in dignified silence, so I very much wanted to get up there and perform something, but could remember nothing except 'When icicles hang by the wall . . .' I opted for being struck dumb, standing shyly under its massive canopy. I could imagine groups of Twenties and Thirties people coming here to concerts and plays in the summer, delicious picnics, high-flown conversations; it was Scott-Fitzerald, Glyndebourne, everything I have desired. It was also almost deserted which was even better. I was reminded of the house where I attempted a market garden, for this had steps descending to a huge lawn in front of the lake, across which similar scenes had once been played by local amateur dramatic societies. How is it possible to feel intense nostalgia for something one has not experienced? I frequently do, as if in getting born when I did had been a punishment for misbehaviour in a more creative time and place. I probably enjoyed it all too much and never gave a thought to the misery of the servants in the attic, as few would. Indulging in fantasy is part of the pleasure of Hidcote, for it is another world.

The Old Garden was a revelation to me also; it was the first time I had properly registered the idea that 'tasteful' can mean excellent – I had formerly used the world in a derogatory sense of dreary modern living-rooms about which here nothing. The colours in Hidcote's Old Garden are all soft pinks, lavenders, light blues, cream and silver. There are lovely musk roses, hibiscus and mallows along with herbaceous plants. It was painstakingly pointed out to me which plants would be there permanently and which be taken into shelter for the winter, and that one part of it was devoted to acid soil loving plants. It is becoming clear to me that a great many blue-flowered plants thrive in acid soil, which was here imported by the train-load and kept up with continual peat mulches ever since. I soon began to think of growing almost everything I laid eyes on, having completely forgotten that I had no room for more than three or four.

'Oh but you can grow things in pots,' MGF told me, thereby spelling doom to my sunbathing area forever. This was such an exciting idea, and still is. The wonderful thing about pots is that they can be moved around, often rearranged like sitting-room furniture, so that the best things are more noticed and those out of season or not very well can be looked after out of sight. Some things take to pots better than others, of course, because they grow and spread rapidly. I have seen lavatera mallows on sale as patio plants, but only in the first season will they be happy in a pot, they grow quickly to about three metres and almost as much across, as the garden centres surely know. At Hidcote they are magnificent.

The Red Border is probably the most directly spectacular garden here, with its enormous dahlias, decorative rhubarb, canna lilies, begonias, and much bronze foliage and some purple too which makes the entirety seem even more red. I deeply envy anyone who has space to create something like this, because part of the point of having 'rooms' in a large garden is that at some time of year there will always be something lovely to look at, likely to be in flower or at its best, whereas parts will only be for spring or summer so you don't have to see a desert from your front window while waiting for your annual show.

For the first time I saw gardening as an art form, which is strange really as I paint and am a keen interior decorator. If Monet's garden is an extension of Impressionism, then Lawrence Johnston's Red Borders make me wonder if he was not a Fauve, for there is in fact some violent orange in there too. Perhaps he loved Gauguin? The whole effect is very exotic and inspiring to say the least. MGF claims that gardening is in fact the highest of all the art forms, and he is very possibly correct. In painting for example, your colours may change over a long period of time, but in gardening this can happen overnight and is, furthermore, not totally predictable when planting. Weather changes everything, winds destroy, various pests can ruin your best-laid plans. If you create a piece of sculpture it at least does not continue growing far beyond your expectations and have to be cut back only to shoot up in a direction you don't care for. And music is silent after its last notes, it doesn't stand there shouting to you that you made a terrible mistake and have to live with it all summer. To create an interesting, beautiful and meaningful garden is a very great form of art indeed.

We sat in Mrs Winthrop's Garden, which he made for his twice-widowed mother, resting from the strong food of impressions in the hot sun. Here there is a Chusan palm, some yuccas, daylilies and agave and other exotics in pots at various times. The view includes trees against other trees, grown to show themselves off from a distance. The feeling is delicious peace and intimacy. Did Mrs Winthrop sit here to do embroidery, read, have tea with a guest, or did these things take place in other, more sheltered corners of which there are plenty? Perhaps she sat here alone, dreaming. I did this for a short while when my companion went on closer explorations of nearby plants. It was good luck we had gone on a rare day of few visitors, Hidcote can be very crowded. I gave myself up to that special feeling of complete happiness which can happen only in a garden. It is outside time, in a state where there are no problems or troubles.

There was much more to see. We strolled along the Long Walk which appears to end in a pair of gates opening onto an invisible road to paradise, you feel you could run down it and fly out into the sky. The hedges are so immaculate and the shadows so sharp you feel like a rather unreal persona in a painting by a British Ruralist. The Stilt Garden is a wonder, hornbeam hedges so immaculately trained and kept, looking just like stage scenery which could be drawn up like flats to change the scene in the theatre. No, such a scheme would *not* thrive in pots.

We left the sun behind for a while and explored the Stream Garden. Dark and woody, ferny, damp, reminding me strongly of a path through deep woodland which I long ago had to walk through on my way home from school, alone, aged five. The smell of rotting leaves, bluebells, the truckle of the beck at the bottom of a treacherous ivy-covered slope, the eerie sound of the wind in the poplars above me I shall never forget. Further along there was a weed-encrusted mere with moorhens and brambles. Little girls do not walk in such places alone any more, for the world has become too wicked, but even then I felt the threat of the place as well as its lure. I began to shiver in the shade of Hidcote, and then remembered another woodland experience. I was early interested in plants, collecting and pressing wildflowers, which was then still feasible and not considered rape of the earth. I sometimes dug plants up and took them home to grow (or sometimes not grow) in pots in the attic, checking them hourly for progress. I recounted to MGF how I had once been chased by Pan.

'It was probably a naughty gardener,' he scorned me, but I told him anyway. I was eleven or twelve then, on a long lone walk and was in a deep part of the woods in the perfect silence once found on scorching days in the deep shade of old trees. I had found some wild garlic, the first I had ever seen, in beautiful white flower with a very strong smell. I began to dig, and became very intent. Wild garlic grows very deep and the task was taking a long time. And then, behind me and high up I heard the loudest and most chilling, mocking laugh I ever hope to hear. A thrilling, terrifying, inhuman laugh. I looked up and around, and froze, so alert if you'd touched me I would have shattered. No, it was not a bird. It came again, louder, nearer, more sinister.

I ran. I have never been much at running, I tended to be asthmatic, but that day I ran, and barefoot for I had left my gymshoes in the woods. Usually rather timid I leapt across stepping-stones, over walls, across thistly fields, through hedges until I reached the main road, more than a mile away. I have never been so frightened nor so strong and fleet. As I ran I heard crashing behind me, there was something there which got left behind amongst the trees. Decades later it occurred to me that the experience had been real panic. The kind which happened to nymphs in ancient Greece. I always feel spooked in deep woodland. Once in an island in the Aegean I experienced something similar when I lost my way on a thickly wooded mountain, but I was no nymph in years by then. I scrambled through thorns and all obstacles to escape until I finally leapt into the safety of the sea.

61

'Well this wood is man-made,' explained MGF, who may have thought I imagined the whole episode, 'look at these ostrich ferns, aren't they just divine? And this purple vinca, this is my favourite of all.' I was still quite glad to get out into the Spring Slope and some light and air. As I said, Hidcote is a place of contrasts.

The Bathing Pool Garden is rather special. Now, it is not kept for bathing except for some newts and water boatmen, but this too reminds me of my childhood. In the People's Park in Halifax there is a round pond with a fountain in the centre, and when I was young crowds of children would swim and splash in it on hot summer days. The one at Hidcote is satisfyingly large, enclosed by sheltering dark hedges against which, later in the year, grow some amazing blue poppies, meconopsis several feet tall and the most desirable colour of all for flowers. They are not easy to grow, but I intend to try in the near future. To produce even one of these would be a major triumph.

Nearby is a lovely little sheltered yard with a covered area with some elegant outdoor furniture, placed for both interesting views and a pleasant secret place to sit and read. There is a *Rhus typhina* in a plantpot, grown taller than mine and not so hugely shady. Perhaps that is the secret, restrict their roots and they bonsai elegantly.

There is another lovely pond in the Pine Garden, with some exemplary containers full of alpines. The first moment I saw these I desired even so much as a common house leek, I would not rest until I had whole groups of them. The mosses and lichens would follow in time; I wanted everything softened with the patina of age immediately if not sooner. I was over-excited no doubt, but so what? When you cannot experience an extreme enthusiasm, you might as well just switch the TV on and yourself off. I haven't had a television for years, there simply is not enough time to waste. I prefer potting, repotting, mulching, weeding, trimming, training and pruning, after-dark slug and snail catching (with a torch and a trowel, in waterproofs if pouring with rain), planting, feeding, watering, and even cutting a few flowers for an arrangement. When my first house leek actually flowered eighteen months later, weirdly and perhaps suggestively, I was ridiculously thrilled. I took the whole container indoors and did a detailed watercolour portrait of it, got it into an exhibition along with some others, and sold it straight away. Which was very satisfying, because the cost of all those plant containers is considerable.

I became incurably addicted to plant-collecting on that glorious day. That I had neither the space nor the great fortune of Lawrence Johnston was irrelevant. I was, like MGF, mentally designing on a very grand scale. All the way back to Leamington we talked deeply about what we had seen, what was feasible, how to grow this or that, where he had seen many of the plants before, where in S's garden many of them would soon appear. It was long after dinner, long after the pub shut, almost dawn before we finally wound down. And this was very good, because a couple of months earlier I recalled sitting on the back step in the sun too weak even to lean forward and pull out a tussock of grass from a plantpot. I had given it a tug and almost fallen over, stared at it in dismay and wondered if I would ever garden again. I had not had the strength to walk about without holding onto furniture or taking a stick with me.

The day after Hidcote I was hauling sacks of compost about, moving pots, digging holes in the edges of the path, forcing out bricks with an old tyre-iron and making lists of what I might be able to get to grow. Some progress had been made but there was so much to catch up with. I could hardly wait for our next trip out, which was to be in the near future. There was so much to see, MGF told me; I had seen nothing yet.

5

Light and Shade

The transition of my garden from suntrap-patio with flowers around, to a jungle of interesting plants, many of which had far from ideal conditions, crept up on me even as I dug with concentration. Everything grew very quickly, fighting not only for space, but for light and air. Something else which I could not predict was a sycamore tree two gardens down, carefully placed between the essential midday sun and my plants. This had been almost invisible when I began my garden, but in five years was taller than the house.

I hate that tree. I should say, I love trees very much, realise their tremendous value to the planet, would if necessary chain myself to one to prevent it being axed. Excepting that particular sycamore. I would cheerfully fell it myself, and nourish daydreams of so doing, dressed like a lumberjack, singing the Monty Python lumberjack song ending with a joyful yell of 'timbe-e-er!'.

It is not as if sycamores were rare, I speak not of a beautiful acer, its cousin, or of a threatened elm. This tree can't be very happy where it is, anyway, shoved in behind the dustbins, its middle branches swishing themselves sore on the walls of an empty factory which it does at least disguise but over which sun once shone. It performs no function in its garden, it sends out seeds which germinate in great numbers for about a half mile radius, probably much more, and creaks threateningly in storms. An ugly polythene bag got caught in its upper branches and was there, flapping and eerily whistling, for eighteen months. Its shadow is long and dense. I want it cut down. A new tenant came to that house recently, and by pure chance I met her just as I was stuffing the car boot with prunings, so to bring up the subject of the tree cheerily was not difficult. Her landlord says it is interfering with the drains and will have to go, but she has pleaded for no major upheaval until her tomatoes ripen. It is September as I write and the tree is still there. Of course, the tomatoes can *never* ripen under its shade but you can't explain things like that to some people. I live in hopes. When her toilet backs up perhaps the sacred tomatoes can be disturbed. I whined to MGF about the increasing shade from one source or another. It was if the greenhouse effect windows were filthy, and soon all I could grow would be fungii.

'You should read Margery Fish,' MGF told me, when I was complaining that my dahlia and my agapanthus would not flower properly because of lack of sun.

'Fish?' He has quite a library of gardening books, but as well as plants he has an aquarium so I was momentarily confused. I need neither television nor fishtank to entertain me, so am left out of glass-box conversations, and now it seemed that my knowledge of great gardeners was similarly deficient. MGF referred to Margery Fish's Gardening in the Shade which, along with her other works, everyone remotely interested in gardening should read.

'You can make a marvellous garden with shade plants only, remember the woodlandy bits at Hidcote.' I did, vividly.

'What, ferns and stuff?' I wondered, not wildly excited. I had some ferns and I loved them, but you can have too many, I thought. In such a small space. With no flowers.

'Oh there's hundreds of things which love shade, beautiful things. In fact, if I had to make a choice between gardening in sun or shade, I'd choose shade.' I didn't believe him, I thought he must be exaggerating. Everybody knows (I thought) that the shady places in a garden grow just grass and some rather boring-looking things plus dense unshiftable clumps of lily-of-the-valley.

'No, I mean it. I'll lend you the book, and we'll go looking into some shade. You will be surprised.'

I have been surprised, largely at what some garden experts will term 'shade'. I have found out by trial and error, or should I say error and error, that what they mean is 'half-shade' in almost all cases. Very few things will grow, apart from moss and some very hardy ivies, in really sunless, dense shade. One or two of the less spectacular euphorbias will do well enough, and surprisingly, Sweet Williams have thrived and flowered for me, and *Meconopsis cambrica* lightens darkness once it has filled all available cracks in the light, but most plants enjoy some light if not direct sunlight. To imagine that glorious flowers will shine out from utter darkness is nonsense, but I must have believed this for quite a long time. For two seasons I was an afficionado of busy lizzies because they will obligingly grow quite enormous and flower profusely in spaces where other plants have died. Meanwhile, I was helping to create even more shade for myself, not knowing how enthusiastic some plants can be.

I nourished an image of a wall covered in honey-suckle and clematis, so a Japanese honeysuckle went in quite soon after the 'Henryi', further down my narrow long strip. It thrived and grew fast and when it first flowered I was jubilant, for the scent of its not very large flowers was heavenly. It never stopped growing, all year round new shoots thrust and twined and climbed and soon it was my pride and joy, except that to my puzzlement, all the things which I had thrust in at its feet, which in my vision would provide an ascending bank of colour, died. This kind of honeysuckle quite soon forms a dense bush, allowing its former year's growth to die off, then covers itself with bright new achievement at the earliest possible moment. What happens then is that you have a thicket of dead tangle sticking out from the wall for about a metre in depth, with heaps of dead dry twigs and leaves underneath, falling onto exceptionally dry soil because the root has drunk all the moisture. You have in effect mulched down all your precious young plants as if they were weeds you were trying to suppress, as well as provided an effective sunshade for them. It was some time before I realised all this.

Another counter-force to success which I had hitherto not noticed was the damage my two cats, Mr Rochester and Emma, were doing. Formerly having had large spaces, a few minor deaths of plants had hardly been noticeable, especially as then the cats were young and adventurous, sloping off to toilet away from home ground. The time came when they were getting on a bit, and although Mr Rochester would go abroad somewhat, he now always came home for toilet purposes, and Emma never left the premises at all. Two cats in a tiny patch are the death of all horticulture. Even more destructive than the five cats, one red setter and five puppies which we had at one time in a much bigger space. I tried many manoeuvres to protect my plants.

Covering up any visibly bare soil with used black plantpots and bricks and gardening tools cut down the area of their operations, but provided ideal conditions for slugs and snails. MGF said he had had much success with plastic pea netting strewn craftily about between plants, but I soon found this a complete torment, because it makes any sort of cultivation impossible. Designing and advising are MGF's forte, not weeding, so he could not have realised that if you can get a trowel down to the soil, extracting it pulls up the netting plus a plant or two and you finish up in tears, cursing aloud. Having spent good money and time on that I then had to spend a lot of time cutting it all out from where the plants had grown up through it, with scissors. Also, my cats ignored the stuff, scratching through it and burying it along with their doings. I experienced deep bouts of despair on this problem.

I spent more time and money on cat repellants. Pepper dust they found extremely attractive. Then I found something with extract of quassia, and although this worked to some extent, the rain washes it quite away so that in damp weather, which is frequent, you use about a bottle a week and it becomes more trouble and expense than replacing the plants. Then I discovered some plastic pods which you tie to the plants, making it look as if everything had suddenly got crossed with chilli peppers. The cats thought that these were toys and spent some time cutely batting them like suspended mice until they got bored. Many of these were later dug up from where they had planted themselves; all were sterile I am glad to report. I kept on discovering them years afterwards when I renewed the soil.

Then I hit upon the idea of retraining my darlings to a cat-tray, an outdoor one this time, with a roof. You can buy these at pet shops, not cheaply, and I bore mine home gleefully. I am sorry to report that they both ignored it, and that when I tried to thrust Emma in through its door she splayed out her feet, laid back her ears, and actually hissed at me. I found the cover quite useful for a long time, for I disguised it with an old roofing tile and stood a potted pelargonium on it and another one in front of it, on the path. Otherwise it was all a waste of effort and yet more money. I did finally prevail, but could not, I think, have managed the matter with both cats. Eventually, Mr Rochester became very ill with kidney disease, and in spite of all treatments for a desperate year, became utterly miserable and I finally gritted my emotional teeth and had the vet come to kill him for me. I do not like the terms 'put down' or 'put to sleep'. Cats sleep such a lot when alive, anyway, that the term is without meaning. I do not know where his spirit is now, exactly, but it is not either down or asleep. I do know where some of his mortal remains are. I had him specially cremated and brought home the ashes, some of which I kept in a small box upon the lid of which I painted his portrait, and the rest was gently dug in at the root of the two clematis.

The next spring, Mr Rochester returned to me as the most profuse blossoming I have ever seen, the *montana* especially demonstrating a wonderful recycling of atoms into glorious life. It climbed up to my bedroom window, framed it, and even came in, where Mr Rochester himself had done when he had been strong enough to climb onto the outhouse roof, and jump. Before there was an outbreak of robberies and a rape in the district, I used to have that window wide open whenever the weather was good, and Mr Rochester would sometimes wake me by standing on my chest and kneading, as cats will. One night, long after his death, the clematis threatening to totally obscure all light, it was so vigorous, I was woken in just that way. I dreamed that he had returned, and then I woke to feel him there, purring deeply and kneading away, claws extended. I heard him jump down and immediately switched on the light to find – nothing. No cat at all. It was not Emma, she was to be found elsewhere, and she never did that to me, she used to sit on my face before I banned her from the bedroom. It was the ghost of my darling Mr Rochester. And in the morning I saw in the mirror that my chest was covered in cat scratches. So if you are at all interested in spiritual matters as well as gardening, do recycle your pets when they leave this world, and see what happens.

So I was left with one cat, and she was eventually retrained to happily use an open cat-tray sheltered under the dense Japanese honeysuckle, where even rain could no longer penetrate, a temporary solution. I now have her cat-tray at the back of the little outhouse, known as the potting shed after I had the outside toilet taken away to make more room for gardening things. But that alone would not have been enough. Cats like soil, and must be kept off it if you want good plants. My stroke of genius, strongly recommended to anyone with a cat/plant problem, is as follows.

Buy some wide-mesh chicken wire. Using wire-cutters, shear off strips about eight inches wide and then bend them into doughnut-shaped pieces, turning in the sharp points. These can be carefully placed around the roots of a plant, and the leaves, and other plants which will then grow in between and cover up the wire. Another formation is a dome to put over young and precious small plants until they get their feet in, when a cross can be carefully cut and the centre bent inwards. Tunnels can be placed in larger spaces, if you have any. No cat can cope with this, and it is hardly noticeable. These flexible cages can be removed, with care, without damaging plants, and if a perennial or some bulbs appear up through it in spring this does not matter at all, the stalks grow up through the wide mesh in no time. Pieces can be moved about and re-used infinitely, lifted out in order to weed, feed or mulch, or to catch snails and slugs. Now, the stench of cat-pee no longer mingles with the scent of flowers, I clean out Emma's cat-tray every day, using some deodorant powder as well, and plants flourish. I think I may have spent as much as ten pounds on the wire mesh, and if your garden is bigger it will cost more of course, but it is permanently useful and if anyone else has a better method, please write and let me know. My beloved Emma is now aged fifteen, and has the same kidney disease which is the scourge of cats, and although I dread her death she too will become a part of the soil which she can no longer manage even to touch, pushing up if not *compositae*, then something which adores alkaline soil.

I may be about to plant another *Clematis alpina*, an early flowering, small climber with bells as near to true blue as any clematis I have ever seen. Emma helped to despatch my first one, but will help to grow the second. Most clematis and dozens of other plants are often described as 'blue' and they turn out to be mauve. Gardener's blue is not painter's blue, for sure, but *alpina* is recognisably blue. My cat is small, peaceful and delightful, so an *alpina* will be entirely suitable. I hope that she will not mingle her atoms with it for many years to come. Meanwhile, she watches me digging and scratching in the soil and I read her mind. 'If you can use the soil, why can't I? There is no justice.'

Damn right, Emma.

So the sycamore and the cats were against an exotic garden, and so were some of my own plantings. The already mentioned *Rhus typhina* in the wooden tub grew so that it made a large patch of dense shade for most of the day, and then the *montana* decided to branch out in another direction and swamped my defensive rose, blocking out more light. In another corner, a *Hydrangea petiolaris* was doing so well it joined forces with the Japanese honeysuckle, creating yet more canopy. The ribes, so delightful in spring, was densely foliate in summer. If I had not got busy trimming back, I would have been completely overgrown, have created a dim cave of startling originality. In fact, if I had acres of space, I would purposely reproduce something of the kind in some specially chosen corner, for it would be a luxurious novelty. But as it was, changes had to be made.

Before that though, I did in fact read up a lot about

shade plants, went to see them growing, and successfully got to grow quite a few. A rather common
euphorbia began to cover a stink-pipe in the corner;
Alchemilla mollis felt very at home; the tamed
Hydrangea petiolaris began to flower more profusely, ferns took hold. Geraniums and aquilegas
competed with one another. MGF relocated a root
of Soloman's seal from S's garden, in exchange for
half of my *Dicentra spectabilis*. And I discovered that
lilies will flower satisfactorily in the shade, although
growing too tall and straggly, if supported they will
survive. Imagine white, pink, scarlet and yellow lilies
appearing for the first time, how they shone out of
what seemed like undergrowth. I had managed to
have the *Dicentra spectabilis* in a pot for two
successive years before it had to be transplanted after
division, and this too lightened my darkness considerably, as did a pot of striped ornamental grass. In
summer, white and pale green nicotiana still glow for
months in shady corners, and the light pink and
white impatiens can grow large if watered and fed
well, in really very dark spots. Bamboo grows in an
old black plastic bucket, which is hidden by a fern
sharing its pot with a *Dicentra alba* and an *Aquilega
alpina*.

But in the shade made by the shade-loving plants,
very little would thrive. I filled in with the ubiquitous
Meconopsis cambrica and a floppy sort of campanula. I was made sad, and MGF and I together,
during one sorrow-drowning evening, invented the
botanical term *'procumbens mortei'*, a probably
grammatical inaccuracy but profoundly accurate
description of some of my plants. We cried until we

laughed, but something had to be done. I sawed off some branches, I cut back, light entered, and things began to look up. Less moss and more blossom, in a season. I began to look at my *Rhus typhina* speculatively, guiltily. I knew in my heart that I planned murder, but I could not bring myself to do the deed for months and months.

Then one day I took stock of just what had not been successful because of the elegant palm-like fronds. There had been at various times: lavender, pyrethrum, wallflowers, gladioli, narcissus, crocus, hybrid aquilegas, perennial poppies, a red geum, scabious, gazanias, irises, and numerous seeds. Almost all of these eventually expired, disappeared, grew very straggly or did not flower. Part of the problem, of course, was the dryness of the soil next to the old wall, the attentions of animals, overcrowding and the fact that the soil was full of large roots, but most of all, the deep shade. It was a hard choice, but somehow it got made for me. My subconscious took over, 'everything went black with a red mist' and I came to with a saw in my hand and a heap of felled branches, staring at a strange golden object in the sky. There was energy and warmth radiating from that mystical orb, and these immediately did wonders for a large proportion of my garden, and myself.

To completely eradicate the stump would have meant emptying the tub and beginning again, which I did not want to do, because the *Iris foetidissima* and the hardy fuschia and *Dianthus barbatus* were going well, as was a hebe. I left it in. Two years later it is sprouting again, as MGF predicted it might, but not in one straight shoot as he said, but many small runners. Regretfully I just nip them off and hope that my rhus will stop waving its hands at me from the grave, like a botanical Stephen King creature. Perhaps it will decide that I am its mortal enemy (which I am) and secretly grow through the bottom of the tub, under the patio and up through my bedroom floor and strangle me one night. I would not blame it at all, for it is morally reprehensible to let something grow and then chop it down.

But that is the brutal side of gardening, and there are many others too. You have to learn how and when to be ruthless if you want anything other than dank jungle. My whole life changed when I became the owner of a pair of good secateurs, saved up for with petrol stamps. That there is anything not cut to shreds is a miracle but, somehow, a great deal of judicious cutting produces more and better plants.

Light and air I can thus introduce, but space, never. A garden this size, for a plant enthusiast, is always going to be overcrowded. If you overcrowd it in the right way, you can be successful.

One has to find out at what time of year each plant will be at its height, and put next to it something else which will be either well past its best, or not due to be a star until much later. This is not of course simple and straightforward, because the weather is not the same every year, only roughly so, but as a general guide it will allow you to have something interesting at all times.

Take for example another small-garden problem which I am tackling for a friend who is not well enough to take on the work. She has been unable to attend to it herself for more than two years, so it is not only in shade but is badly overgrown. There is a roughly semi-circular patch of earth about three metres across, rather deeply shaded for most of the day, full of brave but fruitless strawberries, straggly pink geraniums growing on their own corpses, sadly trailing vinca, sundry 'weeds' including a common sort of spurge which elsewhere might be decorative if controlled (this is a type of euphorbia which spreads too rapidly) and a few worthwhile plants with bulbs underneath. How to make it not only presentable but delightful by next spring? I want there to be something hopeful and beautiful as soon as possible. Mine is the task.

I have just begun taking out all the unlovely ground cover, and discovered a few buried treasures. There are two hellebores, some primulas and a number of bulbs so far, plus a courageous delphinium which may have to be moved, and by trimming and tying back some shrubs there is already more light and the soil is of a good texture, inhabited by worms. A small and largely shady garden, from almost scratch. With cats, and a visiting dog or so.

In the lightest part I may put one of my own hardy fuchsias which is already getting in the way of a new rose, 'Aloha'. When there has been a full consultation about a possible planting which I shall suggest, we may have by next spring, groups of white narcissus, primroses, several fritillarias, Solomon's seal, ostrich fern and an evergreen fern, epimediums, a better variety of lamium than the common one, 'White Nancy' (with pink flowers), because its silver leaves shine out on gloomy days, and a promise of lilies, Sweet Williams and pulmonaria to follow. Possibly there will be room for some polygonums. I shall leave in some variegated vinca, and if permission is given to cut back a branch or two, a *Dicentra spectabilis*, and nearer the path, a *Dicentra alba* along with creeping geraniums and campanulas. Other plants may find a home there as time progresses, *Ajuga reptans* comes to mind for example, which would form a carpet around the narcissus and, with luck, some vivid scillas. But I must not make the mistake of overcrowding, even if the available earth is many times greater than my own.

But you will see that MGF was right when he recommended Margery Fish, for she is a perpetual authority on gardening in the shade (half-shade), and a beautiful sight can be created in what at first looks like a hopelessly dank tip. I find the prospect very exciting, and will report upon progress later in this book. But long before I felt confident enough to tackle anyone else's problems, I still had, and will always have, my own. My education proceeded under the excellent tutelage of MGF. We had a number of expeditions both far and near, and I began to look at anything growing in soil with eyes unveiled. Even a walk to the off-licence was rewarding, except on one occasion when we spent so long looking at various shrubs in the gardens along the way that it was shut when we got there. However spiritually uplifting, physically excellent and emotionally rewarding horticulture can be, it definitely has its sad aspects, and the seeker must be able to weather disappointment of many kinds.

6

Tearing Away the Veil

My stepfather used to state frequently that he could not remember the names of plants, but he could tell the difference between buttercups and daisies because one was yellow. A garden, to him, was something at the front of a house with flowers in it. He liked flowers. But he could never have looked at any of them closely or with anything approaching love, I think, because this would have given rise to curiosity and interest. Perhaps there really are different kinds of people, and some can simply look at a thing and leave it at that. Not me. The first time I saw reproductions of famous paintings, I could not rest until I had got oil paints for Christmas and could try it for myself. That was what happened to me with flowers, and has continued to happen ever since, in recent years becoming almost a fever for more knowledge, for more plants and a continually interesting growth.

When I was seven I wanted to show my stepfather (he of the innocent approach to life) my collection of pressed wild flowers, carefully labelled. I recall very little interest or encouragement for this passion of mine except he did think that the fresh air I got in collecting my specimens was very good for me. I now see that he must have been glad to have me out of the house; he had never been used to children although, as with flowers, he professed to like them. I decided to grow him something wonderful for his birthday, being at that stage delighted with the novelty of having a dad like other children, my own having died when I was three. We had no garden, so I got a plantpot full of soil and a packet of seeds and hauled them in secret up to the very bare and rather dark attic where I slept and played. The seeds were tobacco plants, and bore no cultural instructions. Seed packets were as beautiful and inspiring then as now, but less informative. I suppose they were nicotiana, but they may have been the seeds of smokeable tobacco, as this was during the War, and cigarettes were sometimes difficult to get. There had been talk of people growing their own, along with anything else either useful or edible which could be grown. Digging for Victory, I planted my seeds, all of them, and stood back waiting in excitement.

Every morning I watered the pot, stared closely at the surface, expecting things to happen as dramatically as with mustard and cress. Nothing happened at all, of course, it was very cold up there, there was not enough light, the soil was probably full of virus, maybe the seeds were dead on arrival, who now knows? In that attic my mother used to hang the washing to dry, with the window open, and I slept with wet sheets hanging like ghosts on washlines slung between the rafters. This might explain something about the pot of potential tobacco which terrified me and put me off digging for years. One morning I thought I saw a worm on the surface of the soil, a wriggling, thin, white thing, and then – was it moving or not, I thought I saw it wriggle – another

81

one on the floor. I had a horror of worms and creepy crawlies, instilled by my mother who would kill anything which moved unless it had a name and an identity card.

I had visions of my whole attic crawling with worms, getting bigger and bigger, eating me in the night. This was the end of that particular present idea, the pot ended in the dustbin and I bought him a packet of Capstan Full Strength which was possibly appreciated more than even a very successful pot of growing tobacco could ever have been. The worms were surely threads off the worn sheets and towels, but I never thought of that then. My stepfather could not really *see* plants; he certainly never saw a nicotiana.

In those days there was not much exotica about in Yorkshire gardens and allotments, and nothing at all in pots. I do give myself full marks for experimentation though. To reach out for anything more than a red geranium was extremely daring. The houseplant had departed with the chucking out of Victoriana, and returned with its restoration to the domestic scene.

Incidentally, it was in that same attic that I not only did my first paintings but made my first experiments with a chemistry set, creating some exotic blue-green powder which I am certain was cyanide.

My mother might have been the first person to
unwittingly interest me in gardening, when we lived
in a little bungalow for about a year, deep in the
country not far from where Pan later laughed at me.
There was a tiny garden which when summer came
she dug over, and then planted with seeds. This was
her only attempt ever at gardening, and it was an
outstanding success. There were huge dahlias taller
than myself ('As big as teaplates, those dahlias,' she
told everyone proudly) – snapdragons, sunflowers,
nasturtiums and many others. Even though it was a
marvellously successful experiment, she lost interest
after that, which might have had something to do
with the great number of earwigs and fortylegs and
other terrifying beasties which inhabited her huge
flowers. We went back to live in town, she didn't like
'being out in the sticks'. But I remembered marvel-
ling at all this, I now feel that this was where it began.
You planted seeds, and you got flowers. I have also
always had a great delight in playing with earth and
water, and can still feel the same pleasure in these
elements which I felt when very young. Seeing things
growing was very exciting. I shall never know how
she got enormous dahlias from seed in the Yorkshire
climate just by scattering them, but I remember
seeing the flowers.

Or perhaps it was my Granma who inspired in me
a desire to grow things. She had a patch of lupins in
her tiny back yard, which she treasured greatly. She
collected horse-dung after the milkman and the
coalman and put it around these lupins, and sure
enough, they grew. I remember looking very closely
at these flowers, they were beautiful shades of blue,

every little flower extremely complex, and bees went in and out. I loved these flowers. It is tragic that railway embankments are no longer covered in them as once they were. If I tried to touch her lupins, there were threats. Those lupins were nefast. I wanted lupins of my own someday. But I had *seen* them. I had been lucky, and observed growing plants for what they are; mysterious, beautiful and amazing miracles. A few years ago I had the great pleasure of observing my small grandson intently watching a bee going in and out of foxgloves, his expression of deep interest and wonder a joy to see. To treat flowers as just something to brighten up the front path is an insult, especially if they are regimented and controlled too much.

I know someone (why prevaricate, this is one of my adult children, namely Simon) with a moderately large garden, who has spent eleven years in the army, and his gardening reflects this. The lawn has a razor edge revealing bare soil which instantly loses moisture, upon which no bit of moss or a daisy is allowed or big guns appear, blasting with chemicals in a decidedly military manner. The plants, mostly garden centre bedding, are placed exactly thirty centimetres apart, and if they turn out to grow unevenly or of the wrong colour, they are court-martialled and shot. I took this son, who in only some respects bears out genetic inheritance (he has a surrealist sense of humour for one thing, upon which I depend here), to see some cottage gardens in Burford, in the Cotswolds, hoping to soften and expand his feelings about gardening. And although he acknowledged bright splashes of colour, he could only see lush growth as untidiness. He looked at the houses with their delightful covering of mosses and lichens, and remarked that they could do with cleaning up. He was perfectly sincere. I tried to explain that these growths had taken decades to mature, that they were beautiful, that they protected the roofs, and that a good garden always has something dying even as something else is getting born, just like life. This information was met with polite and eloquent silence. This signifies tolerance of untidiness and sloppiness. What to me is a mature garden is to him an overgrown jungle.

He likes very neat ornamental beds of the park pattern, everything ripped out when over, expendable splodges of colour. If he painted however, it must be observed in passing, it would turn out to be of the *fauve* variety hybridised with John Martin, which uncharitably could describe some of his stepfather's paintings which he rightly admires, but which would do the paintings no justice. This shows that analogies between gardening and painting must not be carried too far. Simon's taste in clothes and furnishings is restrained and subtle, to say the least. People are a mystery, especially if you begin to analyse them and they are your own children as well. Gardening too is a mystery, which will also never be solved, but it can be endlessly explored and thought and felt about, but only when it is not treated as if it was wallpaper by the roll. I attempted to convey some of this as we wandered around Burford on a misty Sunday, me wishing I could afford to live there and he thinking it would be nice if they could get rid of that rotting old stone and build some decent houses.

I was wasting my breath, for this is a person who takes a broom to a couple of leaves on the patio. In the house I am something of an obsessive housewife most of the time, so one could look for the genetic trace element there, as well as his way with words. This is also a person who has asked me and MGF to go and give him some advice about replanting his garden. We are both eager to do this, but I do not anticipate delight at the future results. If we get him to grow a lavatera and the rain weighs it down so that it looks untidy he will be frantic. I know that all the interesting and lovely seedpods will have to be taken off before they are ripe (some of my nigella seedpods stayed on until the end of September because I find them an interesting form) and anything left out to die, such as the tops of striped ornamental grasses, because it looks beautiful as it changes colour will simply not do. I feel that I could have a task preventing him from chopping off scarlet leaves from a Virginia creeper because they were, technically, dead. Getting MGF, a busy person, organised to take a day off to visit Simon with me and start making plans has proved impossible so far, so the task may be mine alone. I will do my best. First though, Simon has to *see* plants. At present, it must be that he is looking at them through a veil, rather a thick one at that. I blame not only the British Army, but garden centres and parks committees for this. I have to confess that I once bought a whole tray of scarlet salvias myself with the idea of 'brightening up' some garden which I was approaching with the wrong attitude (i.e. I did not love it). The salvias died, serve me right. There are still enough people to keep on buying dreadful things and shoving them into soil and not liking the results, dead or alive. Presumably they are rich enough to keep on trying again.

Which is perhaps why garden centres until very recently only offered plants which shouted loud but were not actually that easy to cultivate, and impossible to keep for long. African marigolds, scarlet salvias, the aforementioned blob roses. All need certain conditions and a disease-free environment, frequent care, the right soil . . .?

And love.

It is being said that loud chaotic colour schemes are coming back into fashion, but still, some of the most beautiful and worthwhile plants are rather quiet. A good garden needs some of both, and even perhaps one or two of those very 'good taste' plants over which I have teased MGF at times, so insignificant and with flowers so subtle they are invisible. I think of geraniums with little dark red, almost black flowers, not very many, which do absolutely nothing to lighten the darkness of my garden's most obscure corner. Until, when you get up close, they prove to be extremely beautiful. And they give me the added pleasure of pointing them out to visitors, who invariably stare into the gloom, and I read their thoughts, and they think 'weeds'. If you have a garden filled with only large dahlias it will be the equivalent of listening to a brass band or Heavy Metal all day long. Which, come to think of it, regarding loud Rock music specifically, my ex-army son actually does do whenever possible. Last summer I visited Simon's garden, shortly after some (immaculate) interior decoration had been in progress, so the garden had actually begun to grow for itself. I found not only some thistles which I yanked out with great pleasure (one *must* get thistles out, with hand-to-hand-combat) but in amongst some naturalised violas some trails of *Anagallis arvensis*, perhaps my favourite plant of all. It is sometimes known as poor man's weatherglass, because the little red flowers only open in sunshine, or scarlet pimpernel. It was one of the first Exotic Flowers I ever found growing. In Yorkshire I had never found it, as a child looking for collector's items. But when I visited my Aunty Mary's, in Norfolk, aged perhaps ten, there it was in the lawn, in profusion (this delightful aunt was decidedly non-military in her approach to everything) and I still recall the almost delirious pleasure I experienced in finding it, collecting some, pressing it, labelling it, memorising the name, which is of course why I remember it now, about fifty years later.

'Don't get rid of this, it is a wild flower, not a weed,' I burbled. But next time I visited, it had gone.

Perhaps it will return, elsewhere in his patch of rich clay some twenty miles north of Oxford. I certainly hope so, and if I, or I and MGF ever get our designing hands on that garden, *Anagallis arvensis* shall thrive.

It is besides a very pretty plant, and does no harm at all. Unlike another of my childhood favourites, impossible to cut or press successfully, the immortal bindweed, or common white convolvulus. This must be one of the world's most beautiful flowers. There was plenty of that in Yorkshire, growing on the waste ground, on fences, near the dams and streams where I fished for sticklebacks. I used to stand and stare at it as if it was a miracle, and still do. The day came when I had to get rid of rather a lot of it in order to begin a garden, but I could not resist letting a particularly lush bit of it continue to grow up the pole for the washing lines, where it made a splendid feature for a whole season until there was no room for washing. My method of getting rid of it was quite simple. I cut off what showed, dug out a lot of it, and then laid turf on top of it after which it was not seen again. It dies if deprived of light. But in a border it is a great nuisance, especially if it happens to be the most beautiful, and soon the only plant you have. Someday I intend to grow its even more exotic and less invasive cousin, the morning glory.

I shall need a greenhouse for that; all the window-sills are full. I am told that morning glories are 'tricky'. I wish convolvulus was more 'tricky', it would be such a marvellous garden plant if it was easy to keep in order and did not strangle everything else.

For the present though, my rabbit hole method of gardening will keep me content. It is a mistake to think that a tiny garden will be less than a large one; I have found the opposite to be true. This is partly because of my stupidity or ignorance, of course, in putting in things which became too large, but also because I love to experiment and change things around. In a tiny garden, you know every flower and leaf because you see them up close, and anything going wrong or getting too large shows very quickly.

The landscape is seen through a magnifying glass, or perhaps I become very small myself when I go out there. A large slug on the path takes on the dimensions of a Brontosaurus, an infestation of aphids is worse than a cloud of locusts, patches of blackspot is a Plague of Egypt.

Where the jasmine once flourished too vigorously there will soon be a 'Guinée' rose, the darkest of reds with a heavenly scent. Getting out the roots of the jasmine and Virginia creeper was a good enough digging task to qualify for outdoor exercise, as does hauling sacks of compost, horse manure and grit and bark chippings from the car to the back of the house. Down my rabbit hole garden there exists a large space, plant within plant, several worlds within worlds. The whole of Hidcote is outside my back door, the whole of Kiftsgate, the whole of Biddulph Grange. I am as deeply identified with it as the owners of those great gardens ever were. I know every tiny part of it intimately. I love its soil, I am made very happy when I dig it and find that it is improving, that worms begin to like it, that roots take in it. I am, in fact, taken into another world, a true other dimension when I am gardening out there. I am more truly myself, and yet can forget myself when tending plants. I am the child I was and will always be, exploring the mysteries of the world, covered in the earth from which I sprang and to which I shall return. This is not sentimental non-sense, but a sincere statement about something important which happens between me and plants.

I hope it will be so for as long as I live, and that if you do not understand what I mean yet, that you soon will. Gardening can bring not only misery, torment, strained muscles, an empty purse, despair, sheer fear and anxiety, ruined hands and terrible exhaustion, it can and often brings profound joy, much larger than the garden itself, expanding end-lessly through everything else.

7

Paradise on Earth

Gardening can be Hell, especially in a small space. You have to re-pot several things, changing your scene every spring and autumn, and you do not have a greenhouse full of ready-to-flower plants. So, first take out the plants which will soon die off or be long past their best. Where to put them? You find somewhere safe from your treading them to death, then go to empty the containers of their old compost – what into? An empty compost sack. You save these religiously, using them for prunings and weeds and old cat-litter, taking them to the town dump very often and returning with empty and increasingly horrible old sacks. You unearth a sack from behind a redundant lawn rake and a deckchair, hurting yourself severely in the process but still keeping your cool. You know this is not going to be easy so you mentally prepared yourself in advance. Stay cool, work slowly but steadily, methodically, one thing at a time. Do not rush, all will be well. You hope that there will be no lump on your forehead nor bruise on your shin, that was a bad start but that f******g deckchair will go to the dump too if it does that just once more. You scrape out the dessicated compost, humming a little tune, turn round in such a way that you do not damage the overgrown but still flowering petunias to put down a probably salvageable trailing fuchsia, turn back again for the trowel which is underneath the compost sack which you then fall over. You realise where your trowel is and lift the sack, finding that it is now far too heavy. You get another compost sack, daring the deckchair to suddenly land you one from above, transfer some rubbish laboriously, spilling rather a lot, and get both sacks outside the back gate ready to take in the boot of your car (which you have recently cleaned) to the dump. You spend energy regretting the waste but there is simply nowhere else to put it. You have mulched with burned-out compost as much as you dare and as much as you have room for. All your waste has to go to the dump because there is no room for a compost heap. Terrible. You feel sad and somewhat non-ecological. You suppress the thought that a Zen garden with a few fabulous rocks and some raked gravel and one but only one bonsai would be perfect and that is obviously what anyone with any style and sense would have done, long ago. But, here you are, in the moment, surrounded by demanding plants and jobs, and to live in the moment is a very Zen thing to do. So here goes.

You get the hosepipe onto the pots to clean them out and realise that a scrubbing brush is necessary, perhaps a spot of detergent. You go indoors for the brush, taking in rather a lot of soil onto your newly cleaned floors, go outside only to remember that your rubber gloves are indoors, under the sink. In again, taking in what is now mud because a large puddle has formed from the hosepipe which you left running. You spend energy regretting the waste of water, and guiltily realise that you will be a lot more careful when the water is metered.

You get busy scrubbing out the plantpots, because you know that to leave traces of viruses will doom your tulips, but you also fear that your spot of detergent will despoil the environment, not to mention that it has foamily swamped your saxifrage and miniature geraniums which are happily growing in cracks, but only after years of carefully banking them up with fresh compost underneath, dressing them with grit and charging every visitor to mind their feet, they are treading on plants, whereupon they hastily dance backwards onto something else. You rinse them off and utter a savage prayer for their survival, offering your own unworthy self in exchange for their lives, you are a fool, an idiot, unworthy to touch a leaf of etc., etc., etc.

Now you have to make decisions. Shall the compost from the new sacks fill the pots alone, or should it be tempered with some rather lush horse-manure compost as well? Is horse-manure compost only suitable for open soil, will it transmit horrible bugs and un-named diseases to your precious plants-in-pots? You don't know. You agonise. Will it be too rich, and produce mushy stems, disease-prone over-fed plants? Shall you sprinkle in some soil-pest killer, or do as MGF says and not use such stuff, it is dangerous and damaging? You have used it before without ill-effect, but MGF knows more than you do. You compromise, sprinkling into some pots and not others, in an experimental spirit. You do not however take note of which pots, so the experiment such as it is become immediately invalid. Is there in fact sufficient nourishment in this compost, would a

touch of fish blood and bone meal improve it, or
burn the roots? You don't know. You agonise. You
begin to get indigestion and backache because the
weather is rather chill, it being autumn, a time when
it is more lovely to look upwards at the turning leaves
than downwards at the desperate, struggling, dying
plants, on an empty, tense, churning stomach. You
go indoors to hunt for the gardener's friends. One is a
body belt, a warming and supporting garment for the
mid-regions. It is probably at the back of the bottom
drawer, and probably not. You find it, struggle to
put it on. It fastens with a wide swathe of velcro,
which clings to your pants, your old jumper, to itself,
to everything. Finally, warmed and supported,
layered like Batman with a muddled number of old
tee-shirts, tights, a short and an old jumper, with
your body somewhere inside it, you go to make some
hot strong coffee. This drunk, accompanied by
whatever hearty snack to 'put you on' until dinner
you can find, you go outside again, a cigarette on the
go, spirits rising, to find that it really is extremely
cold for the time of year and that this, plus the coffee
means a trip to the loo. Indoors, which is now
covered in mud and bits of leaves, a trip to the loo
with all those peculiar clothes on becomes a major
task, very uncomfortable and requiring a few words
to Fate, with a clenched fist raised. If you do that in
the middle of trying to fasten a velcro body-belt it
will rebound, and cling to something, perhaps a
towel or the toilet-roll, which will then become
incorporated with your increasingly eccentric mode
of dress. Hyped up with coffee and anger, near to
tears, you go out again. Things are looking up, it is

time to start planning.

But. What to plant with what? How tall will the tulips be? You have planted small tulips before and found them to reach a stately half metre, until a strong wind comes along. You have lovely visions of white narcissus growing up through deep purple and mauve *Ajuga reptans*, but you can't remember if they will be flowering at the same time. You go to look it up, drag out your extremely heavy RHS books, find a breeze immediately comes to blow the pages over, and take it indoors. Well, maybe the information is correct, but where was the garden they take their information from? Wisley. Where is Wisley? South of here, nobody would try to begin a Horticultural Centre of the Earth far north. But what about Edinburgh? How do they get all those fabulous plants to grow in a north-east icy wind-blasted place like Edinburgh? You resist looking for the map and go outside again to try to organise things. It is obvious that you have bought either too much or too little in the way of bedding plants such as pansies and primroses, pink myosotis, and no way on earth will all those 'cram-a-pot-for-five-bob' tulips and daffo-dils find a home. You don't want to fill up the tiny narrow beds with them because their leaves take forever to die off in the late spring, you have learned that hard lesson. Too many large bulb leaves prevent sun and air getting to any seedlings, and they look horrible too. Oh God.

Not to mention any other colour schemes you might have hoped for. Last year, those lovely double pink tulips turned out to be red and yellow striped, they looked marvellous, but it was a fluke and not at all intended. You phoned the garden centre in a ferment about that, but they said they could not guarantee that the workers in Holland never made mistakes. Knowing the fame of Holland for smoking dope I could only lamely agree and retract my issue of a writ even before I had spoken it, and thought that if only they would include one good strong joint with every packet of bulbs, to smoke when your bulbs came up the wrong colour, it would be very nice.

The best and only way to get a good show from bulbs in plantpots is to plant them in layers, getting in as many as possible so that one layer comes up through another layer, the whole topped off with short hardy flowering plants such as the usual pansies, primulas, polyanthus, aforementioned

97

Ajuga reptans, veronica and perhaps young ivies. So you plant and plant, fill up the new pots, and find that you still have a big paper bag of white daffodils left over. This can mean only one thing. A trip to the garden centre, in your ghastly old clothes. This is because it is now late, the 'garden centre' is part of a supermarket, which means that lots of well-dressed people will stare at you as you shuffle past looking like a bag-lady who has mislaid the booze-aisle. You pause at the booze-aisle yourself when you get there through the evening traffic, having succumbed to the idea that by the time you have got this job done, you will have earned a drink or several. You are correct. You forgot to measure the plantpots to go into the chimney pots, or count how many you have already filled. There is only one thing for it, and that is to get (with your bit of plastic) three of those rather nice ceramic pots from the Far East, another load of compost (more expensive here because it is all in smaller bags), plan to use the large one for the daffs and get a couple of packs of extra irises and ornithogalums for the other two pots, there will be just sufficient space for them. And on top one plans to grow more creeping alpines, which will require another bag of grit.

The checkout till is now enormous but you feel great rushes of some emotion not easy to define and rattle back to your car in the fading light, just in time to see a wonderful sunset happening across the maze of roaring roundabouts between you and your home.

Now you must abandon your cool no-rush attitude, you must just jolly well work at speed, efficiently and with fervour. You will have no more gardening time available for at least three days, and you could not live without knowing that all was well with the autumn planting. The film speeds up. Must get it done. And, of course, you want that drink and you have forbidden yourself to have it until all is complete.

In fading light supplemented by the lights from the house and finally a judiciously placed torch, the job is done. All the bulbs are planted, all the little plants have found a place, all the salvageable plants have been wrapped up, stored, or shoved onto crowded windowsills, all the rubbish is in the boot of your car, the future is created. A brilliant show all through winter and an increasingly brilliant show all next spring. You run up the path to the house in which is the fridge in which is the wine and fall over your darling Emma whom you have forgotten to feed.

You do in fact discover that a bump has been raised on your forehead, you discover that your back hurts abominably in spite of precautions, that there is a bruise on your shin, that your hands are cut and will not be smooth again for days, that it is very cold in the house because you forgot to put on the heating, that the Visa slips are astronomical, that dinner will not be ready until around ten p.m. Is this Hell, or what?

No, it is Paradise. You fill the bath with hot water dosed with seasalt, you put your dinner into the oven, you shove all your filthy clothes into the washbasket and hide it, you light the lamps for ambience, you put on your favourite music. You lie in the bath with your second glass on the side, and you relax, you dream of flowers yet to show themselves, you luxuriate in colour and life and energy, a thousand times more reward to come in return for the suffering and energy you have expended as an investment.

All long winter you have something to look forward to.

Gardening is Heaven.

8

The Mystery Plant

It was not yet time to dream over the future growth, or to browse through seed catalogues and indulge in grandiose plans, that year when MGF and I went down to Kew. I think it was probably September, because there was still much to see in the way of flourishing herbaceous borders, but what I chiefly recall about that day was its magical and chaotic atmosphere, its breath of utter unreality which I feel will never be captured again. How is it possible that the day was brilliantly sunny, that I was wearing a long silk skirt, a brown cotton overshirt and a large black hat (clothes for a good summer day in town) and yet we returned to Paddington in darkness around six-thirty? – but at midday we had leaned over the garden wall of one of those enviable Victorian villas at Kew and snitched some seeds from a fully ripe giant cardoon. Surely they cannot be ready until late autumn? There were not two trips to Kew which could be confused, so I just put the facts before experienced horticulturalists who will instantly be able to know exactly when this wonderful day out occurred. Our new greenhouse weather behaves so oddly at times, and I do not discount the possibility that cardoons seed in July. Not that it matters, because I feel it to be entirely possible that certain episodes in life take place in another time-scale, on another world, in this case perhaps the same place/time, approximately Dimension Seven, where my little garden exists. Before I reveal the impossible, I will relate the improbable.

I planted the six seeds which MGF generously allowed me to have, in little fibre pots, and placed them on the bathroom windowsill. One germinated, and was eventually successful enough to be planted out in a blue ceramic container the following spring. I planned that it should be a feature to itself, an exhibition in a pot of its own the following year. I knew (MGF lectured me several times on the subject) that these plants are only really half-hardy, but will become perennial given all but the worst frosts providing they are hardened off over two years, their first year being crucial to their development. I always bow to superior knowledge in gardening matters, or did until lately of which more presently. I placed the pot, after hardening off the small and promising plant daily on good days for several weeks. I got up early to put it out and always took it in on cold days and before dark. I would often go and look at it in its sunny sheltered place, give encouragement, even offering one-to-one counselling if necessary. It had determination and pride, that young plant, for it never told me what MGF may not have known but should have, which is that snails adore the young tender leaves. One after another was gobbled up in spite of my detailed survelliance, slug-killer and magic. I would examine it for these horrible para-sites, find it clear, turn my back for a moment only to find a leaf half-eaten. Don't believe what they say about snails, the bastards are like lightning.

However, each time a leaf disappeared another one and sometimes two appeared, so progress was made. Also, whitefly seem to find the silvery leaves a perfect place to camouflage themselves whilst sucking the life out of the plant, because I did not notice them until it was almost too late. The need for reading glasses in order to see details is a nuisance to a gardener; you put on your specs and see enormous aphids and yet the rest of the garden is a blur and you cannot walk safely. You take them off and everything looks like an early Monet but it is in reality infested with enemies. I now have some half-specs over which I can peer, because bi-focals make me dizzy. I also recommend that you have a strong magnifying glass amongst your tools unless your close-up vision is perfect. This way you may find a tiny caterpillar before it becomes monstrous from having eaten holes in your best pelargonium.

I expended much energy washing and spraying, and my precious young cardoon thrived. For those few of my readers who may not be on intimate terms with cardoons, I should perhaps have explained that it is a sort of enormous thistle, with huge silver leaves, and eventually giant flowers not unlike artichokes (also enormous thistles), very decorative and what used to be known as a conversation piece. Its botanical name is *Cynara cardunculus*, and it is of the compositae family. The buds, blanched by tying the leaves together over them, can be eaten, although I feel that the acres of space needed to do this could be put to much better use. Five times as much earth as I own to provide cardoon buds for a special dinner once a year? I think not. They are very decorative

Gardening Down a Rabbit Hole

flowers and seed heads, and I shall feel privileged should I push up daisies such as these!

I had a young Pakistani girl lodging with me that year, and she dutifully informed me that I had a horrible spiky weed growing in one of my pots. Even after my explanations, she gave it glances of hatred as she walked delicately past, and I am sure this did it no good.

All the next winter it spent on the floor inside the patio doors, leaning perilously far out of its pot, in spite of regular turning, in order to grab what rays of sun penetrated through the then thriving jasmine (which she loved, taking some cuttings for the aforementioned garage). Another spring with much careful hardening off arrived. I am sorry to report that I finally realised that it craved open ground with much sun, and donated it to S's garden, to be placed in the centre of a display of various perennials. There it thrived mightily, but S did not like it and also referred to it as an untidy sort of thing. I have not looked in recent weeks, but by now it should be fully two metres tall if it has not been sacrificed to the compost heap, and holding forth seeds ready to be taken, so that the whole agonising saga can be relived. The improbability is that the plant survived at all. I loved it, wanted it, did my best against all odds. I have seen them in good condition in the centre of displays looking utterly magnificent when the lower parts are well concealed, for they are indeed somewhat unsightly as the old leaves die off. They appear alien and so exotic and contrast to perfection with *Lobelia cardinalis* and canna lilies and orange eschscholzia and lychnis both red and white. Too large for a small space, alas, but it was a good experience for me, and such a triumph. Incidentally the seeds which MGF kept simply did not happen at all.

But all that took place in the other time-scale, before we got into Kew, and it goes without saying that to pinch seeds or anything else from Kew itself quite definitely never even occurred to either one of us. Even had I been tempted, which I was not, I would have desisted scrupulously, not to mention being terrified into rectitude by fear of disgrace, fines and prison. That our day in London began with a visit to a pub may have had some slight influence on the fact that I allowed MGF to steal seeds, and that I accepted six. Looking back, it is remarkable that I did *not* kick up a fuss about pinching a few seeds from the head of a plant with its roots in a private garden, but I did not. I can be a terrible prig at times on matters such as this. MGF has far fewer scruples than me about such matters. He performs linguistic feats such as replacing 'stealing' with 'relocating', but even he would never, ever, I am sure, even contemplate taking anything from such a place as Kew.

We looked at bananas forming from flowers which I said resembled strelitzia, a strange miracle which I had never seen at that stage before. MGF told me that bananas are related to strelitzia, so I felt pleased with myself. I enjoy being perceptive or correct in his presence, I like to see the minute flicker of respect which crosses his features on these occasions. We looked around the aquarium with which he is fascinated, although I think the one at the

Horniman superior now I have seen that. We looked at many orchids and I dreamed my dream of a two-storey heated conservatory built onto the back of the house, post-modern miracle of engineering hovering over all my patch, with a spiral wrought iron staircase leading up to my bedroom which will have been incoporated, complete with glass roof – full of orchids, and strelitzia and insectivorous plants, a place in which to dream exotically although perhaps a bit humid for good health.

We looked at cacti. We looked at everything, each plant received our fervent adoration. MGF was at his most informative that day. I remarked scornfully on the smallness of the aspidistra compared to mine, but was told that there are several kinds, which there are.

At about two o'clock I had to beg for a respite, and we sat outdoors on a bench to eat our sandwiches, watching a group of Canada geese who then watched us before descending greedily to grab what we could spare. MGF told me that they were pests which overbred; I told MGF that they mated for life and were therefore to be much respected. MGF said I was like the Pope, condoning overcrowding by magnifying the very few good qualities of family life. I stepped down, seeing his point as the geese actually pecked our sandwiches when they were still in our hands. And then we went into the temperate house.

We had a wonderful time admiring the ironwork of this amazing conservatory, the spiral staircases, the gantries, the overall design of the place. We fantasised about owning such a structure. I am no longer certain but I think it was in there that we saw

Dutchman's pipes in full flower, quite close up. We saw various kinds of ginger, and I decided that it would be possible to grow a clump of a certain hardy (ish) member of the family which bears yellow flowers with scarlet bracts, and looks like a small orchid. I could not recall its name that day, and I can't today, and it would not have worked in any case. It is designated as a half-shade plant, which was what gave me hope, but the space I had in mind for it is about twenty-five centimetres across, the idea was just a part of *le dérèglement du jour.* And then I saw something amazing.

It was in the base bed, almost central, about half a metre tall, and it had dozens of primrose-coloured flowers. These flowers were about five centimetres across, shaped not unlike the flower of a lavatera shrub, but they had bunches of gracefully pendant stamens, about three centimetres long (at least) glistening like those bunches of glass fibre optics which decorated sitting-rooms in the 1960s. I immediately classed it as an abutilon (hibiscus family) of some kind, but MGF scorned this for reasons I cannot recall, probably that it did not have a central pistil and that the leaves were not asymmetrical. MGF often tells me that plants are classed according to the shape of the flowers, which is true, so this seemed unlikely. Whatever his reasoning, it quickly became acerbic so I decided to wait until I could refer to books or some other high authority. We speculated and argued for some time, and then I suddenly saw that this was some kind of exotic pelargonium.

'Hmmm. Could be I suppose,' he conceded,

obviously slightly miffed that I had hit on this very possible diagnosis before he had. There was a gardener (the higher authority I needed) busily working not far away, a friendly looking soul I thought, and I went to ask him what the plant was, because the mysterious fact remained that this was the only plant we had seen that day without a label. My readers must have wondered why we did not consult the label. The gardener, whom I shall not describe at all in case he gets into trouble, was as puzzled as we were. He went right into the bed of plants to search for a label (absent) and told us that he really had no idea what it was, but that my suggestion of a pelargonium was highly likely. There was something about the quality of the leaves, velvety and of a similar shape, and the quality of the stems, which made us all think this likely, and yet – an abutilon was not impossible. Primrose yellow pelargoniums are rare. We three debated for a while, all intensely interested. The gardener was puzzled that he had not noticed it before, he could not understand how he had missed seeing it, he had weeded that bed.

'You can have a cutting if you like,' he said to me. We literally gasped.

In a hushed but desperately pleased voice I accepted, aware of hackles lightly flittering in the region of MGF. After all, he was the professional gardener, I was just a – a woman! But the cutting, small, expertly achieved, was given to me, amongst glances around for hidden watchers who seemed mercifully absent. My thanks were profuse and sincere, and we dashed away so that I could visit the

Ladies where I wrapped its stem in wet toilet paper, and placed it carefully in the polythene bag which had held my lunch, packed it gently around with dry paper, and placed it at the top of my bag. I felt that never had I been in charge of such precious cargo, which was in fact contraband.

After that I recall ferns, creepers, and other things which by then had become just plants – I could not wait to get home and plant my gift, and to start research for identification. Before that, of course, we had to get it home alive and well. We were obliged to spend time in a pub near Paddington, where every time any person came within a yard of my bag I became extremely protective of it, and by the end of our second pint it was obvious to all that I was probably either a shilling short or a dangerous paranoiac. By that time I was certainly both, and floating above the ground with an ecstatic aura to light my way. I felt privileged, special, elevated to the rank of respected gardener. Once home, I invited MGF in for supper and drinks, and there, immediately, while he did as bid and organised the refreshments, I went outside to mix up fresh compost with grit. After gently slicing across the cut surface of my clone-to-be with a freshly opened surgical scalpel to make sure it had caught nothing dangerous on the train, and watering it lightly with filtered water, in its freshly scrubbed pot, I put it reverently in the spare bedroom which was not too cold, not too hot, not draughty, in fact just right. There were other pelargonium cuttings in there already, and I urged the whole group to make friends and grow roots, and hoped they would be happy. I went downstairs for my second glass of wine and some supper.

We stayed up more than half the night discussing everything we had seen, and going over and over the piece of enormous good luck I had come by, and speculating over all my reference books as to what it actually was. We came to no conclusion, and when MGF eventually swayed off home I went to take a final look at my new, rare gift. We exchanged more messages. It was perfectly happy, thank you, I had no need to worry, it was just a bit surprised that I did not know its name, but even listening very carefully I could not quite catch the words. Thus ended a wonderful day for all concerned.

Weeks passed.

The still mysterious cutting seemed healthy, and tiny new leaves appeared, so I assumed that it had rooted, but I was horrified one day to find a large hole in one leaf. I consulted MGF, who laughingly pointed out a great many little black blobs all over the table of cuttings.

'Caterpillar shit!' he said, sniggering derisively, quickly discovering and squashing some bright green specimens and casually wiping his fingers on his sweater. Humiliated, I went to get my specs and found one or two more of the little beasts. I had never had them in the house before. My mystery plant quickly sprouted another leaf or so, and I thought all would be well. Winter was very evident, but the window of that room was south facing and stayed well above freezing without central heating. I invited MGF for drinks that evening, intending that it should begin early and end early. Bitter experience should have told me that no evening with drinks ever ends early, that it ends when the drink does if MGF is present especially. Thus it was, that over yet another interminable discussion about my mystery plant amongst many other gardening matters, MGF decided that in fact I was probably right, it was an exotic specimen, and that it needed more heat. My bathroom windowsill, also south facing, would be ideal, the humidity would be better for it, and so on. Obediently I rushed to transfer the plant into my somewhat overheated bathroom, wondering madly why I had not thought of this before.

In the morning the plant was dead.

The bathroom is overheated only until the heat goes off at night, and it is a downstairs bathroom and it gets extremely cold until the huge heater warms it again in the morning. I had steamed and then chilled my little darling; it lay *procumbens mortei* in its pot and if MGF had been near I would have killed him.

Eucnida grandiflora procumbens mortei.

But of course, I had myself to blame. I should have thought, remembered that it came from the temperate house. MGF was distraught, apologetic, sad. I tried to pretend that the plant would throw up new shoots if I put it back into the spare bedroom, but it didn't. Death had taken it up, ruining my private dream of being one of the few owners of a rare and marvellous shrub.

What was it? The closest illustration to it I could find anywhere was an extremely rare shrub from the South Seas, not far from New Zealand. It was so rare that when the book was written there was in fact only one specimen of it in existence, the rest having been decimated by strip-mining. I did not write down its name, or the name of the island, but MGF scorned my precious theory in any case. I recently looked it up again, and even the illustration had disappeared from the book, if indeed it was the same book. I can find no illustration anywhere which is anything like the plant. I returned to Kew hoping to see it again, properly labelled. There was no such plant to be seen, it seemed that everything had changed, probably because of the season.

There is a moral to this tale somewhere, in fact several morals. I will allow the reader to self-select.

But I still think how perfectly right and wonderful it would be if the plant suddenly appeared in my garden, popping up where I eventually chucked out the contents of the sad pot; it would be in its right place, down the rabbit hole world, along with lots of other plants which could not possibly survive but which do.

It will be Christmas in a week and yet all my

pelargoniums are still in flower, the nicotiana shows no sign of withering, the tropical fern is rampant. The nasturtiums got bitten by last week's hard frost so they've been cleared out, and I decided I had better wrap up my yucca in fleece, just in case. It is simply too heavy to move, having grown rather large outside this year. Its Chinese blue and white container I have wrapped in bubble-plastic, and the object looks like a ghost, the whole exercise probably unnecessary. Some charming little gladioli are already up and probably in danger, my *Lobelia cardinalis* has put up lots of fresh leaves below the old dying stalks. Odd things happen here in my garden. Sometimes it comes on like a miniature Findhorn, or so it seems to me. And hope is a very fine thing.

9

A Craze for Blue

I met a person who had once had a very large garden in which she had grown flowers for arranging and drying. She had made money from this enterprise which indicates that she knew something of the subject. I was therefore astonished when she told me, not knowing that I too have my 'artistic streak' that any blue flower in an arrangement instantly deadens it. I had never heard anything so preposterous. Under control, I simply said, 'Really?'

Where do people get such ideas from? Blue flowers are beautiful, and bring a kind of celestial energy into a room. Or do I exaggerate? But to say that I like them very much is not enough. I like them more as the years go by; blue flowers are rather special.

I think my love of blue began when I had an enormous overgrown garden outside the french bedroom doors of my flat in a Victorian villa. Most of the garden was legally mine, but the other flats were unoccupied, so it felt like all my own domain. For months there was not a great deal of the original planting to be seen. I did not know if anything had survived the convolvulus and grasses under the old apple and plum trees, and eventually I admitted that most things had disappeared, from what once had surely been a wonderful garden. But in spring and well into summer there were two kinds of amazing

114

blue flowers in profusion, obviously self-seeded prolifically and which in a cultivated patch would have been hugely decimated as weeds. The most amazing blue haze would appear suddenly, as a million forget-me-nots opened in both sun and shade. I do not like to call them myosotis, it sounds like a skin disease. Forget-me-not is sentimental, delightful, and descriptive. Once you have got them you can't forget them easily, they will pop up in cracks all over the place. I have them deliberately growing in the cracks between the flags outside my front door, and they thrive even in north-facing gravel. I call that a valuable plant, because it is beautiful too. It takes two years to flower from seed, but if you take the dried seed-heads and shake them where you might like to have flowers in two years, they are guaranteed to grow there. When my daughter lost a pet cat at her father's house in another part of town, she and I went out and dug up some clumps to plant on the grave in his garden. In return I was given some of his ubiquitous foxgloves, which have been rewarding in the same way. They function as a colourful filler, will offer lots of seedlings which can either be left in situ or transplanted, and are easily pulled out if you have too many or they are in the wrong place.

Forget-me-nots especially seem to have a gift for arranging themselves artistically however; they especially seem to like to grow around the bases of the uglier plantpots, and in the tops of plantpots where unsuccessful plants inconveniently disappeared. When the leaves go mouldy after flowering, you just take them out, there will always be more another year.

The other blue flower is a relative of borage, with rather large rough leaves and hairy stems, but bears heads of small and brilliantly blue flowers for a long time, and also seeds itself everywhere. I had never seen it before coming to Leamington, but it shows no sign of being a delicate Southern Belle, it is extremely prolific once you have got it – which is why I do not have it in my small place now. In the large garden it was nothing but a joy, keeping patches lovely until I had time to replant. This too is easy to take out if you get too many. It lasts a long time as a cut flower, and it certainly does not deaden flower arrangements. Blue of such depth and brilliance has spiritual radiation, and is the nearest in the ordinary world as can be found. Only in dreams and meditations can such colour be exceeded. It is a colour which heals.

I once long ago had a series of dreams of the house which symbolises the self, a house with many mansions perhaps, always big and rambling. This kind of dream is a fairly common experience. When health and luck and energy are poor, then the house is draughty and neglected, dirty; broken windows and bannisters spoil the feeling of security, there are cobwebs and the fireplaces are full of dead ashes. There is something ghastly in the cellar, and from the attic echoes a dolorous howl. If there are any houseplants, they hang down dead. Significantly, glimpses of the garden always show overgrowth and neglect, decay and desolation. In one of my dreams there was a lovely old cobbled yard, but with so much wet moss a person could not stand upright.

But in times of recovery, when good things are

promised and productive work increases, emotional tone rising, then the house is comfortable and radiant. In the dream you see a blazing fire in the hall, stone-flagged and swept clean; all the wood is mended and waxed, the paint is clean and the windows shine. The house is warm and smells pleasant and somewhere your favourite music is playing, perhaps expertly played Chopin *études*, and one window has been left open to let in the scent of roses and honeysuckle from a beloved garden. In such a house I began to go up many staircases, exploring in my dream. I came to a mysterious large attic which I had never seen before, with a small door let in under the eaves, a door such as would not have been out of place in Wonderland. I opened the door and crouched down to go through, and emerged onto a wonderful roof-garden, filled with enormous blue flowers growing in glorious profusion, lighted by a quality of sunlight not seen on earth. This was a kind of ecstasy, and it stayed with me to some extent for days afterwards.

When I look into the heart of a small blue flower now I am reminded of this valuable dream, and this feeling will stay with me all my life. Once seen, this particular blue never leaves the consciousness entirely. If you practise Tai Chi conscientiously, for example, you will see this colour when you close your eyes. So as I began to be drawn more and more into gardening, blue flowers were a desire. They are not usually large, they are often fussy about soil and conditions, not that common in comparison to yellow and pink and white. I have already mentioned gentians and my first disastrous try to have them within sight. I have those two plants at the foot of my camellia, in a tub of acid soil, and perhaps they will live. The camellia incidentally flowered at Christmas and has several large buds. This presents joy and a problem; it is much too cold to sit and paint out of doors and the tub is far too large to bring indoors. I feel it would be sacrilege to cut a branch off this small shrub, but I predict that I may take the last flower and a few leaves indoors to draw, and have to keep it overnight in the fridge if the watercolour drawing is not finished in one session.

The camellia is pink, and really has no place in this chapter, but in the same tub is a thriving lithospermum. This low-growing dense shrub, if luck is with me, will provide a flush of exceedingly strong blue flowers in late spring into summer. I am in love with this plant. It has grown fast since I got it, and this year I have high hopes. When the strength of the sun increases with the approach of May, the blue in these flowers is so intense it is breathtaking. Some of the best examples of it I have ever seen are at Sherbourne, a lovely garden which is sometimes open to the public, not far from Leamington. I noticed on my last visit that there was a small clump of blue corydalis thriving there as well, and wonder if the lady of that manor shares my passion: she is certainly an excellent gardener.

Near her lake in spring is one of the most prolific and marvellous ceanothus I have ever seen. I think it must be either *C. arboreus* 'Trewithin Blue' or 'Italian Skies', more likely the former for it is huge; I cannot name it with certainty here in the middle of winter. A tree, dense and spreading, in the sun, on a corner, near a lake; a fabulous cloud of dense blue flowers almost obscuring its small dark green leaves. For this alone I look forward to a bank holiday in spring when I might be able to go and see it again.

Another of my discoveries is the just mentioned blue corydalis. MGF and I were at a delightful nursery near Evesham one day, spending hours looking round because it is so interesting, and spending not a great deal of money because we are so poor. One could easily spend a hundred pounds there, and not have acquired a tenth of the things one 'must' have. However, I had made a few careful choices, and emerged from one of the poly-tunnels to see a pot full of divine blue flowers, not a strong blue like the lithospermum, not a pale blue, but a glowing blue like a sky after rain. The leaves were small and ferny, the stalks were touched with dark red, and the flowers themselves were profuse, borne on extremely slender dark red stalks, and of a strange trumpet-like formation. The more common yellow corydalis I had lots of spread from a donation from MGF some years before. I did not at first recognise the some- what larger flowers as being of this family. I asked the owner of the nursery about this plant, in a state of high excitement.

I was told that it was only recently discovered, in China, and that it was hardy and easy to grow. I immediately wanted to buy a plant, but I was obliged to order, and wait. The previous season he had sold around a thousand, and this season's babies were not yet ready. MGF thought it beautiful too, and I thought that he was slightly miffed at my finding it first, and receiving much detailed attention from the nurseryman. When I had gathered my plants together and went to pay for them, this lovely man asked me to wait a moment, he had something for me. He went out, leaving MGF and I in a wonderful old potting shed, complete with stove, equipment for making tea, a little sink, and lots of lovely gardening tools and bunches of things drying out. Then its owner returned with two pots for me, one containing a tricyrtis (toad lily), which eventually gave me wonderful purple spotted flowers, which I fortunately painted *in situ* because it did not survive, and the other an *Eomecon chionantha*, which he said might even manage in dry shade, which it has to a point as it has run somewhat but not yet flowered. I live in hopes. They were a gift, from an enthusiast who had noticed that all my plants were chosen to thrive in shade.

He said that the blue corydalis would do the same, but this has finally proved not to be the case. We went back to fetch them and one or two other nice little things, such as a small *Dicentra alba* and a dryopteris, both of which enjoy the shade and manage well in pots. I put the treasured blue corydalis in the front of a border facing east, and for the first few months it flowered triumphantly, and spread a little bit. I followed propagation directions and nipped off one of these and planted it in a pot.

Blue Corydalis (paparolaliced)

The second main plant I put in dry shade and it is not thriving at all, still alive but refusing to flower. Another little clone is even further into the shade and struggles bravely, not far from where its yellow cousin thrived madly for a few years, so madly that I thought the whole garden was going to be swamped with it. I had nourished a vision of blue corydalis being a nuisance, a glorious pest, and giving clones of it to every gardener I knew, but this vision will probably never push through into reality. It would seem, from my reading, that this plant may be of the variety which needs baking in summer (unless this mysterious corydalis is not yet actually in the reference books, which I suspect) much as many iris roots do, and that it also prefers acid soil, or at least neutral soil. This may or may not be true. This particular plant is not described exactly in any reference book I can find, it is probably too new to these islands. Its label names it *flexuosa* which is not in the RHS book, but at an RHS show last year I saw a *flexuosa* which was not much like mine at all. There is always further work to be done on classification, it seems to me. If I lose my plants, I do have two very careful paintings of it, and shall return to the nursery where I first found it, and try again. It is taller than *cashmeriana*, which flowers in summer whereas mine flowered mightily from October, even through winter, came to its best in February and then gradually tailed away in summer but still showed leaves.

The bit I got to grow in a new pot was first of all eaten off by a particularly cunning snail and I grieved terribly, but protected the pot by rubbing vaseline around its rim and placing molluscicide nearby, and the plant sprouted again. It is not possible to approve of blue pellets of poison, but it is impossible for some things to grow without their undoubted protection. One consolation is that no birds come right into the garden to eat the poisoned snails and slugs, because of dear Emma, so death does not lead to death in this case. The new blue corydalis will be quite large in spring, and I intend to try it near the camellia, with some fresh ericaceous compost and a few prayers. Theoretically it should get enough sun there, but if it truly does like half-shade well then that wretched sycamore two gardens away will see to that, because it is still there, bare-branched but threatening. The tomato-growing tenant seems weirdly unavailable for further pleas from me with reference to tree-felling. I must wait. If it comes to a fight for life between an ill-placed sycamore and a marvellous blue-flowered plant, a member of the papaveraceae, then blue corydalis should certainly be given the better chance.

The poppy family are extremely interesting; it is not at all apparent to the untutored eye that corydalis could conceivably be related to any ordinary red field poppy, or to the dicentras, but it is so. Botany contains mysteries within mysteries, and can never cease to be fascinating.

And then one day in an ordinary garden centre I found yet another shade of brilliant blue, small pea-like flowers on what looked like trailing clover leaves. It turned out to be related to clover. The flowers were profuse and so radiant with a perfect cobalt blueness I had bought it before even thinking about where it might live in a rabbit hole. Its name is *Parochetus communis,* although the printed label does not spell it correctly, saying that it is a *para*chetus. It is in fact a member of the leguminosae, which also includes laburnum and numerous other plants, of course. Its other name is the shamrock pea, and apparently it prefers gritty, moist soil, is ever-green, but grows best in an alpine house, because it is only half-hardy and likes half-shade. Which is a shame because it was put into a hanging basket (suitable for containers, transfer to open ground after flowering) where it did well, trailing down to around two feet in length but running out of flowers by July. It cannot stand cold winds (nor can I), so I have wrapped it in fleece (myself as well) and intend to take some of it out and see if I can simulate an alpine house for it so that in spring I shall have two chances of these wonderful brilliant blue flowers. They certainly rival the lithospermum for intensity of colour.

And then I discovered veronica. The wild veronica is familiar to walkers, it grows in common grass everywhere and is very pretty in summer. I had not known that there were cultivated varieties, or that it was a member of the scrophulariaceae and therefore related to antirrhinums; the flowers do not appear to be similar in any respect, but again, botanists have a discourse not readily penetrable to the amateur. I found my veronica in a garden centre, named 'Oxford Blue', described as fifteen centimetres in height. This too is not in a reference book, and besides, in seven months it has spread about forty-five centimetres across, and trails more than that. Said to be summer flowering on the label, it has started to flower a little bit again at Christmas. I have already taken some little clones and planted them in a hanging basket where they seem to be taking root because they are not dead. The flowers are superb, and I suspect that if I had such a thing as a rocky bank, it would soon take it over completely, but to delightful effect; narcissus and lilies could grow up through it at different times of year. The blue of these flowers is like the blue of some trailing lobelias, another of my blue delights, probably the most common.

I have not found this lobelia perfectly easy to grow, which is strange as everyone else seems to have lots of it in amongst pelargoniums. Some summers yes, some summers no. It might help if garden centres would not label the short bedding variety as trailing, and vice versa! I have found the lighter 'Cambridge Blue' the best, it creates a delightful haze around pink trailing verbenas and pink pelargoniums, a better effect than nationalistic colour schemes, I feel.

The best lobelia I have ever seen is at Biddulph Grange, about which place more later. This is a particularly dark blue, which on a rainy dark day in late summer seems almost purple, grown as a thick bedding plant, massed in a border. I do not think I have room for any of this, but I shall certainly try; it would look marvellous around my little creamy rose, where nasturtiums will trail later in the year.

When I was down at Upton House last summer, which is in Oxfordshire but quaintly listed by the National Trust in its handbook as in Warwickshire, I was resting on the terrace when I was suddenly shouted at by a sparse row of surprisingly blue flowers about twenty centimetres tall. With renewed vigour I ran over to them to take a closer look; I had never seen anything like them, although for a few hysterical moments I thought they might be *Meconopsis betonicifolia*. I peered, speculated and puzzled for quite a while before returning to my bench, dizzy with sun and thought. An elderly employee of the Trust was seated beside me, so I enquired of him about these flowers, thinking he looked like an experienced gardener. He had not even noticed them before, and had no idea, which disappointed me a lot, as NT people seem always to be full of facts which you decidedly do *not* wish to know when you walk inside the houses. I have since realised that they (the flowers) must have been dwarf delphiniums, yet another member of that astonishing family the ranunculacea, probably *D. tatsienense*. I would very much like to have some of these, and perhaps someday I shall. Research continues.

And then we come to somewhat larger blue flowers, which of course I crave utterly. Among them of course are the just mentioned *M. betonicifolia*. I am told by everyone except an otherwise wonderful nurserywoman I know that they are very difficult. MGF especially tells me that I would never manage to raise and keep any, and that if I bought a grown plant it would disappear without trace in a single season. I do not know whether to regard this as a true prediction, a challenge, or the gypsy's warning, that if I actually succeed with them he will kill me. I have in mind a group of three *M. betonicifolia* for my acid-soil tub, because for these it is completely essential. And here is some information which the perceptive reader or the knowledgeable gardener may already have realised or known, though I have never heard it said before this autumn, by myself. This is: almost all blue flowers prefer acid soil. I realised this when at Hidcote and again at Biddulph Grange, admiring the lobelia, and also being surprised at the prolific patches of gentians which shone out between ferns. The soil there is decidedly acid, I would say, the whole place is built upon moorland, rather away from the alkaline Peak District by about thirty miles.

Not unlike Halifax, although I never saw a single gentian there. They were probably too Lawrentian for Halifax people, as they were in my childhood at least. Not that I adore Lawrence (D. H.), being female, but he wrote a very good poem, Gentians.

Meconopsis are close cousins to the papaveracea. I found a small plant labelled 'Blue Bread Seed Poppy' at a small herb garden near Southam. Whether it meant 'Blue Bread' or 'Blue Seed' I could not be sure, but I bought it, of course. The vendor informed me that it was a lovely blue flower about five centimetres across, and that it would seed itself everywhere, and needed sun. I planted it in sun. I waited, and waited. One day it bore a pale blue flower, and the next day it was dead. I have not seen it since. It was about thirty centimetres tall and very fragile-looking, promising to be as prolific as its cousin the *M. cambrica*. Not in my garden. Perhaps it too needed acid soil? Was it the opium poppy from Tibet? MGF tells me that the really blue poppies are not the opium poppies, although I saw a photograph of an entire landscape covered in them illustrating an article on the drug trade: bright sky blue. MGF says they are really the mauve ones, about which more later. Anyway, I don't like poppy seeds on bread, they are constipating, and so are opium medicines, I just want the blue flowers which clear the brain without bad side-effects.

And here I must mention once more the most splendid of all blue flowers, which are sparse but splendid against a dark hedge at Hidcote, in autumn. *Meconopsis grandis*. Fabulous. Very tall, very elegant, very beautiful, very blue.

And very, very difficult to rear, so says MGF.

Well, we shall see about that.

Meanwhile, the campanula is not doing too badly, growing in corners and cracks almost dark. Coloured slightly towards mauve, but in the right light, blue, definitely blue.

Blue as a colour does not deaden flower arrangements, by the way. It is the proportion which matters. You need a lot.

10

Derry & Tom's?

There have been various kinds of impasse in my garden, but the most painful are when I devoutly wish for more and different plants, and even I can see that there is no more room. Once I was so insane with lust for gardening that I even began to think it a good idea to put my small bench sideways on the path to the back gate so that I could stack up some steps in its place, upon which I would balance at least a dozen new plantpots. I had a young man staying here at this time, who had gone along with my enthusiasms with great politeness, even to the extent of taking photographs (at my request) of various areas, to show changes as the seasons progressed. That he could not detect some of these arcane views of seasons says not only that he is not a gardener, but a young man who likes to sit in the sun, eyes closed or behind dark glasses, reading. The look of dismay on his face at my change-of-furniture ideas was piteous. I shall call him J.

'But you've only just made that nice little table!' he all but whined. It was clear that there would not be room for it in front of the bench if I moved the bench. I sighed.

'It is lovely,' he continued, 'to sit out here on Sunday mornings with one's coffee and the paper, and it is also lovely to sit out here on warm evenings with a bottle of wine, isn't it?'

'Well yes, that's why I made the little table but . . .'

'We won't be able to get past the bench to put the rubbish into the bin outside if you put the bench there. You'll have to go out of the front door and all around the block.'

'Yes. I do see that. It is just that I have been wondering how I could get more alpines in here, they're not very tall are they, some are almost invisible, do not take up a lot of space you see, and also . . .' I could sense that he had stopped listening. He had got past the hot flush and had gone pale, a dangerous condition to argue with. When I get on a roll about gardening when J is present, he can take just so much. I sympathise. I feel just the same way on the rare occasions on which he feels he must tell me how brilliant he is at designing cars, and that he is in the top five per cent of the world's intelligentsia, and that when he can afford a house of his own it will certainly not be a small Victorian terrace, and so on and on. I always give and take with my young friends; they don't generally call me a crazy old bat and I generally don't call them spoilt selfish fascists.

So I either had to give up the idea of getting any more plants, or think of some other plan.

There was the small space at the front of the house. An estate agent would call it a garden, but it isn't. It is a metre of dark red concrete, with a hole in it over the cellar window, and a short path of stone flags which I unearthed from beneath some vile sparkly tiles. To disguise the concrete I have covered it with gravel in which grow little plants here and there. Ferns have appeared through the cellar grating, from mysterious spores, and look delightful. Doubtless more delight could be registered if there were more plants. To find the earth beneath the concrete would be a very major undertaking, I felt. And the concrete keeps the damp out of the foundations. Also, by the look of all the other 'gardens' on this row, nothing very good will grow because it all faces north and is something of a wind-tunnel furthermore. My next-door neighbour has a honeysuckle and a *Hydrangea petiolaris* doing quite well, but I do not need to repeat those two. To my amazement he also has three thriving bushes of lavender.

We both have quite a lot of a creeping plant known as 'mind-your-own-business'. I think it is a moss, and in passing must mention that it makes an excellent, hard-wearing and brilliant green lawn which needs no cutting, according to a certain person in Warwick, where MGF and I have visited at her Open Garden days. She has a lawn sweeping grace-fully right down to the river's edge, and most of it is this 'mind-your-own-business' plant, and we all three enthused greatly about it. I must visit again this spring to see if it is in fact hardwearing, because the growth outside our mutual houses here in Leamington was blackened by frost recently. My neighbour came out and scraped it all away, very kindly, managing to do away with my creeping geraniums and one or two alpines at the same time, but, like an Alan Bennett character, 'I said nothing'. MGF has often urged me to put tubs or planters out there at the front, and I can quite see why. One either side of the small bay could look wonderful, although MGF's idea was to plant a clematis against the wall, in a large half-tub.

'No. Flat no,' I finally had to say, having thought about it. There was a good reason why none of the other houses had handsome swanky tubs and pots outside. This was because people just come along and steal them, plants and all, in the night. I had thought of somehow bolting them to the floor or wall, but I could imagine that the frustration that might cause would easily be turned upon my car, which is in any case often vandalised. Leamington is a nice town with a few mindlessly spiteful people in it from time to time. To place what could easily amount to a hundred pounds worth of containers filled with interesting plants was to 'ask for it'. Besides which, the watering problem in summer was large enough for me just keeping all the pots moist at the back of the house. I would have to bring watering cans through the house, spilling on the polish and the carpets – no, MGF, no, sorry, no. He looked at me mournfully, like a whipped dog, which is what he does when he can't have his way with other people's property or lives.

So where was my garden going to? How could I expand my little universe?

As I pruned the *montana* soon after it had gloriously flowered, sometimes from a stepladder, sometimes by leaning out of my bedroom window with a pair of kitchen tongs to grab sheaves which I then hauled towards my shears or secateurs, I was struck by inspiration.

Below me, of course, was the roof on the little outhouse, or 'potting shed'. After the clematis had flowered, and the parthenocissus tried to take over against some of my best efforts, and the *Passiflora caerulea* failed to do much in that direction yet again, not surprisingly, there was a total waste of space!

I would have a roof garden!

Now, underneath the thick growth there are sheets of some corrugated stuff made of something I don't know what, simply placed across lightweight beams which go across the top of the brick walls. How strong all this is it is not possible to say without testing it to the ultimate, and you only know you have reached that when it creaks horribly and caves in. I could see myself being landed with a situation I could not handle without expensive professional help. It was daunting.

I did not impart my plan to MGF because he would have immediately wanted me to plant some exotic palm about a potential five metres across, having built an enormous planter on top of the roof. That I thought of this first and dismissed it as lunatic is beside the point, he would have gone on and *on* about the matter. He is quite visionary at times but I think impractical. I began tentatively, and even this presented enormous difficulties.

I had some blind irises which had never had enough sun, so I dug them up and then cast about for a possible container. I had one of those brown plastic urns in two pieces, but the bowl part toppled off the base at the slightest touch, so I could visualise that in a high wind an unsuspecting visitor might be damaged by a flying bowl of irises, and this was not good. To be able to reach this roof, not very high but very awkwardly placed, was a big problem. I got the stepladder from the cellar, through the kitchen, around the corner into the dining-room, through the french doors and down the path, carrying it above my head so as not to damage any plants, erected it as near as I could, but from the top it was still not possible to reach the roof. I was already exhausted, and sat down at my little table with some coffee and cigarettes, reflecting that J was right about the necessity of having this little haven intact, in this place. It catches the sun and is sheltered. But, the bench is in the place where the stepladder must be to reach the roof. A scene from Laurel and Hardy ensued during which I am glad to say all the damage was to myself rather than any plants.

I had to move several containers, and play around with the very crazy crazy paving to find a balancing place, and finally I could go up and see what was what. A jungle was what, about a foot thick. To get at the secateurs, in the outhouse, entailed removing the stepladder again, and then replacing it when I was certain I had got everything I would need for this job. The whole garden now looked a shambles, with clematis trimmings, a ladder, buckets of compost, bits of containers, tools and roots all over the place. A less determined person would have simply turned from it all and gone to the pub, and do not think I did not consider this option. It was a blazing hot day and I know a pub with a large back garden where claustrophobia is unheard of, and they have draught cider. I called myself a mad fool, a masochist, and continued.

It was useless to fill a container and then take it up the ladder, because I needed one hand to balance myself going up steps, so the answer was to first place the container in position, and then take up a partly filled pail of compost and transfer the contents with a small pan, before putting in the irises. This entailed about ten trips up and down the ladder, but the plan worked. I inserted the edges of the container under the strong clematis so that it would not blow or roll off. I effected something similar, and larger, at the other side of the roof, with a much larger square container, hiding its ugly green plastic under the clematis and parthenocissus, placing it over a beam and not too far into the middle of the roof. In this I planted a lovely little cream patio rose, with some verbena and a *Petunia* 'Surfina Purple Rose', which eventually grew almost ninety centimetres, flowering profusely over the edge of the roof. Also in these containers went some trailing nasturtium seeds and one or two sweet pea seedlings. Another sweet pea was inserted in a small pot from whence it found its way to the light and climbed up to my bedroom window.

A disadvantage to all this is that trimming and dead-heading is only possible to a degree, by standing on my bench and clinging onto the faithful *montana*; there is no room to keep a ladder out there, and it would in any case be an invitation to any thief determined enough to cut his way through the rose thorns. I feed with liquid feed in a watering can from my bedroom window, and water with a hosepipe with a spray rose on it, inevitably drenching myself but who cares? This spring I have in mind at least

135

two more similar containers, possibly with more veronica, and certainly with some more of these wonderfully vulgar trailing petunias. You can see my roof garden several houses away , and my immediate neighbour is already very impressed with the show.

I would now never waste a flat roof which could be reached at all; the view from my bedroom window is lovely, because it is directly below, but a display could also be splendid on top of a garage at the far end of a garden, as they often are.

I think a hanging window-box might be a good idea as well. It is surprising what can be grown in a window-box. MGF is the arch window-box artist. In his town flat, three floors up, he has an amazing collection of plants on the sill.

First he leaned out to drill the brick, so that he could fasten on his plastic containers with chain, all too aware that if one fell from that height it could mean certain death for his plants – and any person underneath of course. Then he planted what would seem to be a ridiculously large number of incompatible plants, for example, *Iris foetidissima*, sweet peas, pelargoniums, geraniums and others all together. They all live together so far, and he smirks triumphantly about this. I shall be slightly more circumspect with my window-box if I make one, with the aim of achieving more than mere life, but a show of flowers. MGF reluctantly concedes that trailing petunias are rather wonderful. I shall buy several and present him with one or two; he will not refuse.

The problem with an upstairs window-box is the watering, of course, as the bathroom is downstairs. I manage to water the roof garden with a carefully controlled hosepipe, but one can hardly aim up to the bedroom window. Perhaps I can devise some kind of sprinkling arrangement? The mind riots when desire calls.

Now, in winter, I am thinking or dreaming about ways to strengthen the corners of this little roof, or perhaps all of it, by inserting steel rods across to spread weight, so that I can place a container on each available corner, and possibly even another container in the middle. I have a lovely hardy fuchsia which would arch beautifully across the other vegetation, coming into flower somewhat after all the main show and continuing with flowers until late in the year, depending upon frosts. And of course, doubtless influenced by MGF's insanity, I have another extremely bold idea, possible for the summer after next.

I was given some banana seeds for Christmas, along with a cute little pot, a plug of peat and some slightly jokey instructions. I have followed these instructions, and the seeds are now thinking about germinating, on top of a painted wardrobe which cleverly houses the central heating boiler in my bathroom. If the temperature difference between night and day is not too great, then soon I shall have little seedlings. I intend to raise at least one of them into a banana tree, for they can be grown outside in England, with lots of care and good luck. The top of the potting shed is not exactly sheltered, but it does get all the sun, and if I train the clematis to form a screen for the prevailing wind . . .? Having once dreamed of growing exotica inside my transformed bedroom, how triumphant it would be to be able simply to put a hand out of the window and pick a banana for breakfast. If you don't experiment, you never get results. I may not in any case, but it will be fun to try.

Bunches from
Santa Lucia

Another possibility is a verbascum. They flower all winter and smell heavenly. I have a vision of floral scent drifting in even during frosty moonlit nights, when I leave my window open at night. Such a shrub would eventually, like the banana, get too big for its place, but this is the case with most shrubs in tubs and pots, one day you have to rethink the whole thing. But gardens grow anyway, and have to be rethought from time to time, nothing is permanent, all is in a state of flux. This is the nature of everything, so why worry too much about what a plant will look like in seven years, if it is in a pot? Or perhaps the hebe which thrives but does not flower, because it gets too little sun, would enjoy a rooftop position? This is, of course, my most sensible idea to date. Something lovely will thrive up there. I wonder where you can get steel bars from at a low price? A demolition site seems likely. This is the sort of project which can begin even when the weather is too harsh to go outdoors much and kneel down in slush. Steel rods, some more containers, young shrubs, compost, all can be gathered before planting time arrives. And perhaps a lightweight folding step-ladder? More expense, but think of the joy of it all. I do, often. When enthusiasm for gardening takes over, your spirit never plunges completely into sunless winter gloom, there is always something to live for. A sunny inner vision may be a good treatment for SAD.

And soon, very soon, once more we shall be able to go out visiting exemplary gardens.

11

Rain or Shine

In what felt like the pit of the year's stomach MGF and I decided, that soon we must, but must, go on a trip. We longed to see extensive signals from beneath the still-cold earth, we pined for new plants over which to exclaim in joy; we needed, not new pastures but new exquisitely cultivated gardens. Over too much alcohol we made bleary plans, arguing viciously with great tact as to where we might venture. MGF sometimes takes the attitude that he has seen everything, quite forgetting that on other occasions he states grandly that every garden is utterly new every morning. He is not a driver and has no inkling of distance and not a clue about time and the stress of driving hundreds of miles just for a day trip. We decided to save some of the finer Irish gardens, and that of Beth Chatto in deepest Essex until some more suitable date, and aim for somewhere possible.

We enjoy houses as well as gardens, of course, so pointed ourselves towards Worksop in Nottinghamshire, where the now famous Victorian semi of Mr Straw can be gazed at in detail, and is within a short distance of Clumber Park. We were very intrigued as to the garden at Mr Straw's, and hoped that it would be appropriately planted, although even we did not expect too much for the time of year and the windswept location. Neither of us had ever been to Worksop, although I had long ago lived south of Nottingham (where I had the landslide, the forest fire, and finally grew very edible broad beans), so we did not know quite what to expect.

I always envisage myself wandering around gardens in a long skirt and a large hat, slowly because of the heat, somehow speaking in slightly elevated tones ascending into a spiral of lofty amusement. This actually never happens because I am not a reincarnation of Vita Sackville West, Virginia Woolf, any of the Mitford girls or the elusive Violet Trefusis, who all probably stumped around in boots guffawing in butch mode anyway. I have managed to dress in my favourite fantasy clothes on many occasions, but always somehow end up by shrieking like a fishwife with a Yorkshire accent, marring the image considerably. What more often completely ruins the entire scenario is when it is utterly necessary to wear dark blue nylon cycling anorak and trousers with heavy boots, gloves and scarf tucked inside because it is pouring with rain, blowing a gale, and very cold indeed. I am used to it by now of course, intrepid and courageous in my search for garden experience, but the awful whistle which such water-proofs give off as you walk does not speak the same language as whispering silk. I have traversed some of this country's loveliest gardens in some of the world's ugliest clothes. But not to be sensible is to court pneumonia and almost certain death.

On our trip northwards it was already blustery and raining in the early morning. We said nothing, having grimly packed the waterproofs, two flasks of hot coffee, numerous and various sandwiches, and I secretly wondered if, should I have 'a drink' at lunchtime, would it have worn off before it was time to drive home? There was a vast and hostile tract of motorway to negotiate. Twice in one day.

We got there with surprising ease, trying Radio Four from time to time, discussing various planting schemes, and I listened yet again to a detailed list of reasons why it was so ghastly gardening for S, the spiritual lady who allowed snails to overrun (if that is the right word) her patch, because they were 'little beings'.

'So are AIDS viruses and tapeworms and pirhanas, did you tell her that?' I asked him, cackling triumphantly. I hate killing things of course, but snails . . .!

'No. I wish I'd thought of it, but it wouldn't have made any difference. She gathers them up in a bucket and then goes and releases them onto Newbold Common, where of course they die of starvation because they are used to garden plants, not just grass. She's mad.'

'Yes I know. Can we talk about something else?'

'Oh God, am I being a prat? Am I boring you?'

'Yes.' Driving against big lorries in driving rain in an old if powerful car with an obsessive passenger always makes me slightly irritable. So in this way we passed the time, and stumbled out of the car in excellent humour in spite of our funny clothes bravely worn, and into Mr Straw's house, about which I should not tell you much here. Go and see it for yourself, the details are in the handbook of the National Trust. It is extremely fascinating. The very small gardens were an instant time-trip into the past. Here was the atmosphere of my childhood.

There was still the original outside lavatory, the only wrong note being the addition of a washbasin with hot water source, otherwise it was perfect. Perhaps someone should paint a *trompe d'oeil* spider on the whitewashed wall, I was almost always watched by a spider as a shivering child. Then, for the time of year, authentically, there were very few plants. In the 1940s, and earlier, suburban and town gardens had left behind the grand schemes of the past in which flowers at all seasons were mandatory, and had not yet got into the current swing of planning for the same reason. Most people had Dug for Victory, which had meant vegetables, flowers had been a luxury. I knew there would be lily-of-the-valley, bleeding hearts, marguerites (as we used to call large white daisies), the occasional pom-pom dahlia, perhaps some golden rod and a red hot poker, one or two ferns and some snapdragons. Not a great deal else, probably, but every plant treasured in its season, and shown off against privet, at the foot of which nothing grows but a pile of twigs. It was heaven, it was my Granma's garden, my Aunty Mary's garden (she had bachelor's buttons as well). What made it perfect was the path, made of cinders. This is an experience not much available these days, but once all gardens had some cinder path somewhere. Gravel is much posher, cleverly laid brick was unusual, cinder you just sieved out from the ash and clinker from the fire, and put it down in place. It was, truth to tell, quite nasty in summer when it got into your plimsolls and sandals, and you got told off for treading it indoors of course, but it was part of *how things were*.

We crunched on history, and then in a mood of hyperbolic nostalgia went off to Clumber Park. I resist an account of our time spent in Worksop, admiring one or two extraordinary old buildings, and steeping ourselves in the gloomiest possible atmosphere of a seemingly defunct mining town which had once thrived. Perhaps on a sunny day even Worksop cheers up, I shall never know.

Clumber Park was not inspiring to us either, in that weather, but we did find a wonderful nursery there, filled with many unusual plants. It is well worth a visit if you are in the district. After much discussion I bought a little blue *Iris setosa* which has not yet announced itself happy. Perhaps I should move it into my acid soil tub, with more sun? – If I can find it.

Clumber Park was curiously devoid of spaniels and other people, we were almost the only visitors mad enough to want to expose ourselves to the weather in search of enlightenment. The sky was fabulous though as watery light broke through the dense cloud from time to time over mysterious forest and an enormous silver lake. We both agreed that in many ways, garden viewing in the rain is at its best, because there are no crowds, and many plants have especial beauty in rain. The Japanese take this view of gardens in rain, and have several words, none of which I know, for different qualities of rain. I wonder how they say 'bucketing down'?

MGF and I came home in a non-stop rainstorm, fast along a flooded, crowded motorway, and upon

arrival home quickly became jubiliantly drunk. I
would not have missed such a day for anything. But I
hoped for better weather for our next trip, as who
would not?

Some time later, we decided to take ourselves
north again, and see for ourselves the restored
gardens at Biddulph Grange. I had lived not far from
there for several years, but at that time the place was
doing duty as an empty haunted house in overgrown
gardens. It was rumoured that hippies squatted
there, took lots of drugs and had all sorts of good
time denied to the young mother I still was. I wish
now that I had investigated the scene, to be able to
compare then and now.

In 1923 it had become a hospital, but by the 1960s
had sunk into dereliction. Now, great efforts and
huge expense had been put to use on the gardens, and
we had read about it in several places. Forgive me if I
have mentioned this place before; I shall probably
mention it several times unless severe restraint is
exercised. No person with the slightest interest
in gardening could resist relating impressions of
Biddulph Grange, more than once.

We got there without a fight even though MGF's
mood struck me as being somewhat impenetrable.
He indulges in periods of non-communication which
are intensely frustrating to a companion who lives
like a hermit, and therefore wants to catch up on the
last two or more weeks' very interesting news. He
objected to every radio station I could find, so we got

there in silence. At least it was not raining – until shortly after we arrived and then it poured, in thoroughgoing Staffordshire style. The only thing which happens more in Staffordshire than driving pelting rain is driving freezing wind. I recalled how glad I had been to leave that very strange area of the country, and took a deep breath and offered a silent prayer of thanks to whatever it is which rescues women from slow death by boredom. We had waited a long time to organise ourselves for this day, it must not fail. My waterproof nylon trousers whistled cheerily as we paid for our tickets, emerging onto the terrace, stately under moody clouds. There were no other tourists visible, so wordlessly we both fantasised about being the owners of such a spread, taking a daily constitutional to check out the progress of the recent planting. I can report with joy that it is all going incredibly well.

MGF raised his aristocratic profile slightly, and even as the rainclouds darkened his spirits rose as we discovered more and yet more marvellous, almost unreal garden creations. Without the National Trust none of this could have existed, and whatever we may think of marmalade costing twice its normal price with half its usual flavour, or Beatrix Potter table mats, we must remember that everything in this universe has to be paid for, under the eternal rule of light and dark, the kinetic balance of good and evil. The gardens were good.

We restored our circulatory systems by walking first up, and then down, a magnificent avenue of wellingtonias. We were then able to be amazed and speak in hushed tones of Butlin's on a skateboard when we turned up in a temple containing an Ape of Thoth. I speculated about the original owners being freemasons, indulging in black magic, and the *fin de siècle* rage for anything theosophical. The ghost of Annie Besant snuffled past me as I gazed with mingled horror and amusement, I swear. This was a grotto par excellence, but its impact was considerably lessened after we had seen the whole show.

The stumpery, with its ferns, for example, is a sculptural marvel which Graham Sutherland would have wept over. The total effect of old upturned trees properly placed is matchlessly grotesque and beautiful, very gothic and eerie. The necessary labour to realise any of the ideas to be found at Biddulph is surely considerable. There is a small pyramid there, over the Temple of Thoth, for example, which would certainly take more than a few visits to Great Mills on bank holiday weekends. Such extensive and intensive landscaping is quite beyond the scope of the usual.

The cherry orchard struck us as being completely original, unlike any other orchard. It is extremely formal and controlled, not the kind of approach which usually inspires me to eulogies, but this concept, which can be viewed from Italy also, most perfectly filled space, function and aesthetics. The base of each tree is concealed in a perfectly trimmed mound of *Cotoneaster horizontalis*, but even more amazing, we thought, were the long swags of *Clematis flammula*, trained along chains and smelling deliciously like almonds. Presumably almonds could not be grown, but this inspired suggestion is one that any gardener with space could emulate easily, as a kind of post-modern room-divider. This kind of delight is only possible to those with plenty of garden space; even I could not manage to use this effect in a rabbit-hole garden.

The dahlia walk reminded me of my father-in-law's allotment long ago in Yorkshire. He was an expert in dahlias, specialising in blues (which are, of course, mauve) but had some rather remarkable cactus types as well. The blues he gave me filled the whole of the rather horrid front garden in the modern estate with the nasty neighbour, and, being so full of large mauve blooms for months on end and nothing else, put entirely to shade her more chaotic colour-scheme. It was from him that I learned about winter storage of tubers, and disbudding in order to obtain larger flowers. The Biddulph dahlias are magnificently vulgar, as dahlias should be. The gardeners there must go around disbudding them rather often, some of those flowers could have won prizes for size.

I cannot with honesty usually enthuse about rhododendrons, but I have to concede that there is a good collection of particularly beautiful specimens here, the greater part of the planting being for acid soil, they cannot be ignored. More interesting to me were the numerous flourishing gentians and ferns.

It started to rain in earnest so eventually we sat sheltering for a while in the cloistered upper terrace in 'Italy', which also overlooks the dahlia walk. This, we decided, was the perfect setting for a particularly tense and witty exchange from a play by Noel Coward. We ourselves were feeling slightly too damp to sparkle, but were quite happy simply taking in impressions. After a while, we went to China.

I think this part of the tour changed MGF's life, perhaps not completely for the better. Ever since then he has dreamed volubly of water gardens. A pond-change overcame him, but not until we felt its full impact from the reproduction Chinese temple, after we had stared in mingled adoration and horror at a life-size golden bull, improbably placed in a shady corner near the path. There is also a sculpture of a frog well worth looking at, which changed my mind about the desirability of sculptures in gardens. If I can have a frog like that one I shall be delighted. I would never kiss it, however, in case it changed shape.

There is a lake here, not large, but marvellous enough for MGF to actually go down on his knees, he said so he could peer more closely at the golden fish swarming around: I think he was worshipping the entire scenario. The architecture of the temple and bridges reminded me completely of Taoist temples I had visited in Hong Kong – that and willow-pattern plates of course. There are painted and tiled verandahs, little bridges, lilies, ferns, a landscaped hillside with precipitous paths, and every view from every point is perfectly proportioned. After very long silences broken only by sighs, MGF switched to rave mode. Without a doubt, even a tiny garden was now incomplete without some exotic water-feature.

'If I had a small back garden like yours, I'd dig it all out into one great pond, right from the back step to the back gate.'

'But you'd have to take the rubbish out to the

Gingko
Lotus
Water hyacinth
Carp
Frogs
Temple bells
Camellias
Ferns
Willows
Acers
Rushes
Kumquats
Bamboo
Bridge
Temple
Umbrella
Boat

Notes:
Former outhouse to be
disguised as Taoist temple.
Damp course strengthened around lake.
Dining-room converted to boathouse.
Replace hosepipe with lifebelt.

Garden:
2 metres × 3 metres
plus path 0.8 × 6 metres
(approx)

Chinese-style water
feature based lake

dustbin by punt!' I laughed. 'And besides, the sewers run under the earth, just think if they backed up, you'd have a lake of . . .'

'Oh you! You have no imagination!'

'On the contrary, I can imagine it all only too well!'

'But just think of the reflections.'

'The floods during a rainstorm.'

'Think of looking out from the kitchen window to see lotus and water hyacinth.'

'Drowned grandchildren floating.'

'The tinkle of a small fountain.'

'The row of fisherman's boots by the back door.'

'I'm going to talk to S the minute I get back. She is going to have, not a small pond, but a lake.'

'She is going to have hysterics. I think I might now if you don't shut up.'

But this was not possible, I was slowly drawn into his mind-lake, and did seriously wonder if it might be possible to have a very small pond. I knew it wasn't, there would be nowhere left to stand, but the idea was compelling. I had decided long ago that it would be too expensive and troublesome to have an electric pump driving a small fountain, but there was no harm in dreaming. MGF was mentally building a small bridge over S's pond, and bamboo was already three metres tall. If you go to Biddulph Grange then you will perhaps be able to experience its effect for yourself. The use of a pocket calculator is recommended while making rapid plans for completely redesigning whatever garden you have in favour of mainly water. And, of course, with the climate changing, there is also the risk of serious infestation from mosquitoes, water-snakes and crocodiles. MGF was so taken with his vision that even these became glamourous. Water-garden psychosis can be quite a serious condition. It is not entirely curable, but may largely burn itself out over a number of years. You have been warned.

And still it rained, and rained, and added to our pleasure; there truly is something special about gardens in the rain, when they have been designed to enjoy it and there is somewhere for humans to shelter and sense water surging through ferns, cleaning the lake, delighting the fish and dropping sonorously from temple bells on to nylon trousers and healthy waterside plants.

I drove us back at speed through hissing fountains, glorying in the rude wake of heedless trucks, aqua-planing intrepidly homewards to my warm parlour, supper and wine and long hours of over-excited discussion, reference books opened all about us. The hideous waterproofs dripped dry over the shower-rail and outside, forgotten, the happy snails munched wetly on.

12

Turning Pro.

As my gardening knowledge expanded, gradually at first and then rather faster under MGF's tutelage and the scourge of bitter experience, it seemed that S's gardening knowledge had stopped dead. This is strange, because in several other areas she is very clever. She plays the viola, is fluently bilingual, is trained medically and in several areas of alternative medicine, initiated and edits a successful journal, is a fully trained motor-mechanic and knows for certain that God exists. In matters horticultural she suffers from information blockage to a severe degree. MGF bored me to tears on several occasions releasing his frustration over working for her, and he himself has wept blood even as I watched in dismay, simply because she has her own ideas about gardening, and will not shift. With regard to horticultural matters, she is like the man who is reasonable and pleasant until he sparks the ignition of a car, and then it is 0–60,000 BC in six seconds. She may well be pure spirit as a healer, but put a trowel in her hand and she becomes a dangerous megalomaniac and drivelling sentimentalist at one and the same time. There was a period of time when I did her garden for her, MGF being much preoccupied elsewhere. I told him, 'I am merely keeping your seat warm, you may return at any time and I think you should.' He was adamant that this would not be possible, and now I appreciate his point of view.

If gardening in general is a true test of patience, then gardening for S is the ultimate character test. That she is not buried in her own compost heap is a monument to the work-on-the-self of all who have so much as dug out one of her dandelions. Which she loves. And the daisies, and the clover, and the buttercups and so on. As if you and I did not also love all these wonderful flowers. It is a matter of where they are loved, and in what quantity. I am very grateful that she has no nettles to tie herself to in order that they shall not be cut down. I have to extract great barrowloads of goose-grass when she is not looking. She thinks that its disappearance means it is out of season, and I am able to tell her quite correctly, that like Arnold Swarzchenegger, it will be back. If it is not kept well at bay, of course, it is capable of dragging down small trees.

I gently refused to take charge of her vegetable garden. Not only do I not feel sufficiently confident to do someone else's vegetable garden, in a ruthlessly organic manner, I know that it would be incredibly hard toil for little reward. I have heard MGF out many times on the subject of this vegetable patch, which he initiated. It has since been reconstructed by another of S's minions, or friends, or friendly minions, but basically it is just no damn good at all. For a start, it is under an enormous old pear tree which bears only wasp-ridden bullets and should be cut down, but S adores it in a thoroughly Druidic manner, so it has to be lived with. It soaks up most of the available sun for a great part of the day but it looks so beautiful from her balcony when in blossom and causes her literally to sing and whoop with joy. That a slowly growing *Acer palmatum* would be more decorative and even more beautiful and would cause her to go into epileptic fits of ecstasy is a thought to be dwelt upon only briefly, because the pear tree will be cut down only over her dead body. Both MGF and I wish.

Her garden had hardly been touched except for regular if inexpert lawn-mowing for about two years. All MGF's thoughtful plantings had become over-grown, blown askew, dragged down by killer weeds or eaten by invasions of giant snails, grown fat upon whatever had dared to show leaves in the vegetable patch. But this awful patch was the most overgrown of all. I offered to at least dig it up and create yet another compost heap with all the truly dreadful seedy old cabbages and weeds growing there but she would not hear of it.

'That is rocket,' she cried, pointing at some pleasant wildflower towering over the dandelions, 'a wonderful source of – of . . .' and here she trailed off, torn between various minerals and vitamins, which in that state even rabbits would have scorned. The flowers of rocket are quite pretty, as are various brassica flowers. I do not think that brassica in flower tastes good, but she swears she eats it. She also claims to make wonderful salads from chickweed but I notice no diminishment of this pest except where I pull it from the flower-borders and shove it out of sight under other compostable matter. After the first real rain this spring, the vegetable garden shot up to around three metres in height and I had to cut a swathe through it to get to the compost heap. I am very glad indeed that I disclaimed all responsibility for it. I have had a very tough job getting the shrubberies and borders into shape. First came the pruning. And meanwhile across the back road my own little paradise was not being neglected. I removed my gardening clothes only to shower and sleep, if I could find the energy to get upstairs.

I did nine or ten hours every week for her all spring, and still there were shrubs to be cut back and sorted out. I made a huge pile of branches separate from leaves and weeds, instructing her to hire a skip because the amount was far too great to stuff into a car; a dozen trips would not have cleared the half of it all. She has not yet done this so it looms at the side of the house stacked in an old bath, looking rather ugly. She was very distressed that I refused to chop it all up and compost it. I explained that it would take at least ten years to rot down and that there would be more next year. She, being an excessivist in all things finally accepted that we must simply get rid of it, but I think she goes out at night and prays over those dead branches, hoping that they will spring into life again. She is in principle correct in that nothing should be wasted. I was ready to explain that, in fact, all molecules do eventually return to the earth and that even if the old branches were burned at the town dump, there would be an excellent source of potash which would colour up flowers intensely, and would somehow, someday, somewhere, be recycled. Where did she think it would go – Mars?

Then there is the matter of the east-facing flower-bed. It is shaded by branches despite my rigorous pruning, and totally stuffed with tulips. For a few weeks in spring these tulips, aided by liberal bluebells and wayward vinca, look very beautiful. And then of course they drop their petals, their stems must be shorn forthwith before seedpods appear, and their leaves wither horribly and there is absolutely no room in which to plant anything else. I have unearthed from between these tulips some peonies and fennel, and managed to insert a giant helianthus and a globe artichoke which she had been given and commanded me to find a place for, and also managed to snitch in a few annual seeds after getting rid of the tulip stems and finally, the horrible horrible leaves. Tulip leaves must be left on to wither because they feed their bulbs by photosynthesis, but they should never be the main feature of a flowerbed while they are so doing. I began to detest tulips for a while, and even now I think they must be severely controlled. I would like to grow a clematis and a rose up the fence behind them, but she thinks that all the flowers would go over the other side towards the sun. She has a point.

But not the answer, because I hope to plant a wider version of my rose and clematis scene along the fence, purposely choosing plants which will not be likely to go much above two metres, and train them rigorously sideways. Consultations have taken place on these and other matters. MGF is correct; she must be the worst person in the world to work for. One does exactly as she says and then, when you have carried out instructions, she gives utterly contrary information. I am informed by other gardeners that this is often the case when working for other people.

All garden owners who are not intimately involved with their own earth 'have no idea'. They have vague intimations of how they wish their garden to look at all times of year but are incapable of conveying this information to the gardener. I have at least got her to the point where some kind of plan will be drawn up, but if this will actually take place I do not know. Making a plan takes considerable effort and time, and I would be expected to do it 'in my spare time', which is to say any time when I am not actually on her land slaving away in the jungle. This I will not do. She must make the plan 'in her spare time' and then we shall discuss it further. I may, in fact, decide not to work for her after all; it is a discouraging business, gardening without horse manure, and using compost which turns out to be utterly stuffed with seeds of lettuce, beetroot and possibly rocket. Amongst my annual seeds there are millions of lettuce seedlings which she says are wonderful because she can eat them, but she does not, and they block the light from more interesting plants. I dispense with thousands and still they come. I would not be a professional full-time gardener for anything in the world excepting I had full charge of it all. It is taking all the full extent of my psychological skill and patience just to restrain myself from strangling this person, and to take everything she says with a pinch of salt.

There are far too many shrubs in the garden and some need to be sacrificed. We agreed on that. We walked around it all together and what happens? She is so fond of every one that none of them, finally, except one ghastly twisted little holly can be sacrificed. That I correctly pruned a flowering currant immediately after flowering causes her to go into paroxysms of barely restrained grief. That the hazels along the shrine walk are killing one another in an effort to get at the light, meanwhile shading fruit bushes which cannot even be reached for great clumps of golden rod does not make her wish some of them to be extracted. She wants a wild garden. I think I shall leave her to have just that. Perhaps.

And perhaps I shall be able to exercise wisdom, and continue creating order out of chaos with one hand, while with the other fending off her un-educated remarks with a smile of understanding and agreement. It remains to be seen.

I am not certain that in the end I can even pretend to be on a wavelength with someone who cannot understand that every sucker and wayward branch of a rather mucky lilac should be preserved, while at the same time they expect delightful plants to flourish underneath it, in neat nourished mounds. If gardening my own little haven for numerous speci-men plants is gardening down a rabbit hole, then gardening for S is like trying to create a Gertrude Jekyll miracle in between a Capability Brown land-scape of trees and shrubs which are meant to look natural but which are manifestly arranged, and a 'wild garden' which is in fact waste ground.

O goddess! How bloody depressing!

Unfortunately I found some similar contretemps in the small but pleasant garden I began to restore and replenish for my friend who was too ill to do anything for herself. She has now been dead almost half a year, but in the spring I had the very sad satisfaction of seeing some of the plants she had chosen to see for herself, but doubtless knew she never would. We had discussed it thoroughly and she had drawn up a plan. I cleared all the stuff she hated or which was encroaching too far, nourished the earth with sacks of old compost and fish-blood-bonemeal, and began to replant. All was going splendidly.

Whenever she was well enough, in between bouts of drastic therapy, she was taken by her very caring and attentive partner to buy new plants, and these went in to her specification. I gave her the address of a wonderful fernery south of Stratford-on-Avon, and several ferns began to get a hold in shady difficult places. The excellent fernery gives good advice as to the best places for their plants, and these were followed. A *Dicentra alba* was given a home.

A neighbour who was also one of her very closest friends gave her a clump of Soloman's seal, and this

went underneath a rather nasty conifer about which
the less said the better. I did not even mention the
possibility of getting rid of it at that stage in the
garden's history, not far from a small edifice which
had its own dreadful poignancy, although once it
had been a source of amusement. It is a small
headstone which made a delightful piece of garden
sculpture. Everything straggly was tidied up, especially the usual rampant geraniums, and I took several
carloads of rubbish away. Lilies were bought and
planted, her favourite colours, under my special cat-
proof cages. Cats and dogs of all shapes and sizes had
previously thought her garden a public toilet, and
this I planned to stop. She delighted in crown
imperials so two groups were planted which could be
seen from the house. They were carefully placed
deeply enough, on their sides, on grit and in prepared
earth. I saw them begin to grow in spring when I went
along with a large clump of penstemons, 'Blue
Grape', and some heavily scented sweet pea seedlings which I had reared from seed.

The next time I visited, her daughter was there and
the crown imperials were not. She and the caring
partner, now a kind of guardian for her adult
children, had been busy in the garden. Where were
the crown imperials? She didn't know, there had
been nothing there but weeds. My cages had gone.
Some of the tulips were still on their way but others
had been chopped off. I was asked 'what those spiky
things were?' Lilies, I replied sadly, taking in the
general drift of the situation. I gave her two calla
lilies in a pot with instructions to keep them wet. The
daughter told me that in the autumn she planned to

Gardening Down a Rabbit Hole

dig everything out and nourish the soil and begin
again. I did not ask why, nor make much of the fact
that her mother's plans had been coming along
nicely and that it was a lovely idea to continue them,
as a memorial. My heart had sunk and the energy
had gone out of the project. The garden, after all,
now belonged to the daughter, and the dead have no
say in things.

I planted a few annual seeds and quietly informed
the neighbour, who was watching everything with
keen interest, that I did not think I would be coming
again, because there was no point. The neighbour
said that she would 'have a few quiet words' with our
mutual friend's daughter, but I knew that nothing
would make any difference. It takes more than a few
quiet words to change the style of an ignorant
gardener, especially perhaps a young one who has
never really got in touch with earth, light, shade, and
seasons. This girl's preoccupations were quite other.

I have not been there since, and no longer nourish
fantasies in rather bad taste, about the ghost of my
friend watching me cause her plans to take shape.
Life goes on, and doubtless if there were such things
as ghosts, they have better things to do than drift
around the back garden approving or otherwise
about what is planted where. Although if I ever find
myself to be a ghost, I think that I would drift into
my garden immediately, hoping desperately that
someone with hands more corporeal than my own
would please, please dead-head the roses, and see
that the honeysuckle was not allowed to strangle
everything else. I would be right in there with the
ghost of my darling cat, pushing up osteospermums

and somehow making anyone else who tried to root out my favourite plants very very uncomfortable indeed.

I would become the employer, and the gardener would have a nasty time trying to please me, for a change. Every time they went near my lovely Japanese painted fern, a deathly cold chill would creep up their back and they would have to go indoors to get warm. Every time they even conceived the idea of getting rid of the lilies, they would begin to itch abominably, all over, and have to go and take a shower and change, and forget gardening for that day. And if they left my 'Grenadier' dahlias out in the autumn frosts they would not sleep until they made the digging-up and dry-wrapping their very next task.

I feel no intimations from the Other Side that all is not as it should be, and so my conscience is clear. I do not in truth believe in the Other Side, although the concept of parallel universes has always exerted a powerful appeal. In one parallel continuum, the true owner of that little garden is still alive and still not doing much with her garden; it is full of her daughter's empties from the continual party which takes place there, it is the exercise ground and toilet for all the lurchers which seem to be constantly visiting along with their traveller owners, and a mangy Apso Lhasa creature from next door, and all the cats from everywhere. Dead bikes clutter its paths, no lilies sprout spikily, the crown imperials are still a figment of longing, and I never went near the place with my do-gooder hat on. Nor ever will again. I have my own enormous plans to effect.

This year is going to be the Year of the Mixed Border, with an emphasis upon hot colours. This idea I conceived long before it was declared to be the coming fashion in the magazine articles, and I take this to mean that I am in tune with the *zeitgeist* as so often before. What this means in effect is that people think you are merely following fashion, which is quite annoying. What must happen, then, is that down my magical rabbit hole I must create the most glaring, showy and hot border that anyone has ever seen, and do it well. Subtlety is out of the window, good taste is put to the back of the mind; colour is the thing this year. I shall invite Dame Edna to visit, and she will swoon over my gladdies. The shade will be filled with utterly startling and enormous begonias with flowers fifteen centimetres across. Incense passion flowers will overcome people with their alluring and even sinister scent and suggestive curving stamens, enormous nasturtiums will make stodgy people come over all peculiar, and the roses will repeat flower in great bunches, even at the same time as exotic lilies stain white silk blouses with pollen as powerful as saffron. I shall have to exchange my gardening lady straw hat for a Dorothy Lamour sarong, and wicked Caribbean cocktails will be served, perhaps to wicked Caribbean people who will be intoxicated also after dark by the potent scent of heliotrope, nicotiana and darkest purple petunias, the ones who let you know that they belong to the Borgias of the plant world, cousins of nightshade and love apples. I shall, in fact, create yet another type of typical English garden.

13

Receiving Admiration

When everything in your garden is lovely and the flowers bloom in amongst interesting foliage, you do not always want to admire it alone. Your great wish is to share the fruits of your labours. You secretly long for a bit of admiration yourself, or at least astonished approval for what you have created. It is surprising how very little notice people truly take of other people's gardens.

I have on many occasions had visitors come to the house, who I presumptiously surmise were dreading the experience of claustrophobia often induced by tiny houses (overstuffed hovels as in 'newly-built modern house'), who have been instantly over-whelmed by the sensations of spaciousness which I have managed to effect, once the front door in the undoubtedly too-narrow hallway is closed and I have breathed in to allow them to pass. And then, on warm days when the french doors are open, and they see the view into my garden, the various decibels of appreciation begin. These are not unwelcome, indeed they are embarassingly gratifying, my chin goes down, my eyes close, I make *moues* of denial, I mentally blush with pride, and also champ with irritation very quickly. Because what these kind and wonderful people are actually expressing is a slightly patron-or-matronising attitude that I have managed to make such a ghastly little house habitable *at all* and, furthermore, managed to get so much stuff to grow in what is clearly too small a space, call it garden if you will but you could hardly turn round, darling. Humph! I feel like a chimpanzee who paints in a modern abstract style when faced with this attitude; or like a woman. Not done well but done at all – this is the miracle. Murder brews in my black heart.

These people are not usually the ones who know anything much about plants. They like to see splashes of colour. They screech with delight at a red gladiolus, at an even redder giant begonia. When the roses are doing their very best they even ask me the names of the varieties and what I feed them on (bacon and egg breakfast, goat's milk, occasional Mars Bar) and how did I train them in that fan shape (hypnosis), but they completely fail to even notice a one and a half metre tall cimifuga just coming into bud, with its very beautiful bronze leaves and deep purple stalks. A kind of selective blindness is very common, I am sorry to relate. It is pitiful.

'And what is this queer thing?' I am asked, of my rather prize specimen of *Abutilon megapotamicum* 'Variegata' with its multitudes of interesting scarlet and yellow flowers. I delight in reeling off its name, and so often have the reply 'wish I'd never asked'. I wish they'd never asked, either, if they aren't interested. I used to point out, when I had a mallow, that it was related to abutilon, and yet this information rarely astonished. That it was also related to my hibiscus also failed to astonish, although when I first

Abutilon megapotanicum
variegatum

learned this (from MGF) I was wonderstruck, enchanted, illuminated. Most people just want blobs of
colour and a whiff of scent from a garden. To
provide this at all times of year, in a tiny space, is
exceedingly difficult. I have done it, I do it, and it is
really quite a task. So to have people come in
January and simply cast a glance at my few early but
wonderful bulbs and the seeds of *Iris foetidissima*
and the various patterned leaves making everything
alive out there in the cold mist is completely up-
setting at times. I wrap up warmly and go out there
and spend considerable time knelt on the harsh
gravel looking closely at scillas, and deriving

enormous pleasure from the process. To walk past a
terracotta pan full of brave scillas is like walking past
the Mona Lisa while intent on deciding where to dine
that night. Which people also do.

So many people cannot tell the difference between
a pot of common daffs and a pot of rather special
white narcissus. White, with very subtle creamy
trumpets, with several flower heads to every stalk,
long lasting, scented, stately, pure. To say 'very nice'
after I have pointed out such beauty is something of
an insult, to the flowers of course but I empathise.

Almost everyone walks past my pot of sage. It is
ordinary sage, but it is grown not for the delightful
aromatic leaves, because I rarely have pork to eat,
but for the truly beautiful and delicate purple
flowers. They are elegant spikes against a cream
painted patch of wall, only just less than a nuisance
as to taking up space down the narrow path. They
attract bees. I have taken a spike of sage and studied
it, and painted it, and find their small but intensely
lovely flowers a great delight. This is a member of the
labiatae family, related to nettles, the grandly named
lamiums, those brilliant salvias of municipal parks,
and doubtless the purple sage of the cowboy songs. It
is also a plant with therapeutic properties, good for
the digestion for example. There is a red-leaved
variety and a variegated-leaf sage too, and if I ever
have a large garden I shall immediately plant a patch
of sages. But it will not have as much meaning as this
sage bush which has lived and grown and flourished,
offering me flowers for seven whole years. It was a
tiny seedling when a friend gave it to me and now it is
sixty centimetres tall but has been severely pruned

every year, and still it grows, even though I have not given it any fresh soil. Just thinking about it makes me want to go rushing outside and renew its compost.

It finished flowering just as a patch of another very common sort of plant, in another pot, began to open, and this is montbretia. This plant is a most vivid and delicate and exotic creature, which has many lovely cousins including the half-hardy freesias, and some more subtly coloured varieties in salmon shades, but even the commonest form is beautiful. Sometimes, because a plant is common we simply cease to notice it; when grown as a special pot specimen, crocosmia-montbretia, whichever you know it as, has presence, it glows. It does spread rapidly in open ground of course, but in a pot you simply take it out, cut it in half and repot it every two or three years and give away the other clump. It will then give you a lot more flowers the next summer. And for a few brief days most years it shines out at the exact opposite end of the spectrum to my nearby pot of sage, seen from the doors or seen from the back gate, different at all times of day but always fabulous. And people walk right past; how sad for them.

Most of my ferns receive this cursory inspection, although ferns are undoubtedly marvellous, and very varied. The exotic ribbon fern now in a pot of its own near the french doors is growing fast and its light stripes attract attention. I explain that it is not usually hardy but that I have had this five years without needing to bring it indoors, and am rewarded with 'Oh'. I feel intensely protective about this marvellous fern, and give it some special praise all to itself when the offhand visitors have gone. The same applies to my lovely Japanese painted fern; it is quite visible at the foot of 'Genie' hardy fuchsia, but it is taken for granted as growing matter of no distinction. I point it out and am again rewarded with 'Oh'. A rather flat 'Oh'.

I must learn only to discuss interesting garden matters with informed and sensitive souls, and be content with empty remarks from others. But it is disappointing not to be able to share pleasure. Be prepared; even the most intelligent and intellectually driven people – the artists even, and the musicians – may be garden blind. Like my stepfather, they may call everything with colour 'flowers', and everything else 'leaves'. This is not in itself incorrect.

Explaining simple things to non-gardeners without sounding patronising is an art in itself. Most visitors of this kind will reach out for the nearest flower, yank it cruelly towards their noses and sniff. In bright sunshine or a cool breezy day, this usually yields nothing, which I know, but they will still exhale as if with gratification. Best to say nothing but I can never resist telling them that the scent of most flowers is strongest after dark, and some have no scent at all until night. And yet some of the exceptions, such as the marvellous custardy scent of heliotrope and the heady chocolate scent of *Cosmos atrosanguineus* I point out in vain. It usually takes at least three massive lungsful for anyone to be able to name the scent, by which time I feel irritated with them and suggest making tea.

'Green China or Earl Grey?' I ask equably (as if they might be able to tell the difference).

I noticed someone the other day gazing in puzzlement at a tuft of pale grass growing in a plantpot, and then saw a dawning light.

'Oh, you grow grass for your pussy cat to nibble?' 'That is Bowles' golden, and I wouldn't mind her nibbling a bit but unfortunately she prefers my red rush there,' I replied. Again the 'Oh'. So, it is bright pale grass, but it is beautiful and has the virtue of not spreading. I explain that my *Juncus effusus* is not accidentally twisted but is grown precisely for its decorative spirals, and then it really is teatime. The male fern at the foot of the rose got a round of applause for its sheer size; I must be content. No matter that all male ferns are enormous and everywhere. Some people simply never noticed them before, undoubtedly confusing them with common bracken. And do I do any better when I go visiting?

Well yes, since I was tutored by MGF I do not simply cast my gaze around, I look and study, and derive enormous pleasure from discovery and comparison, enjoy being startled by unusual combinations. I wonder if the owners of the gardens wish I had remarked on the lush nature of certain types of passiflora, considering that this year is so hot and that these plants enjoy the heat? Do I fall short in praise of day lilies flowering in deep shade or in brilliant sun? I hope not.

Sometimes, of course, it is the owner of the garden who simply does not know or notice what they have in their own earth. S, that truly frightful garden owner, invited me (as a very nice hostess of a birthday party, I might add, the garden owner is really a complex part of a person's character) and during the alcohol-free proceedings I slipped out to see how things were growing since I had chucked in the towel.

Devastation. A tower of sweet peas had obviously been a marvellous sight, but she had not bothered to cut off any of the pods, nor feed nor water them, and they were crisply dessicated, whereas mine across the road were flowering rapidly, again and again. She had not trimmed, dead-headed nor watered anything except the few pots on the patio, and these were indeed flourishing nicely, just as I had intended. The pelargoniums were okay, as they enjoy near-desert conditions, but they would have borne more flowers had they been regularly dead-headed. The solanum was rampant, so rampant it was strangling the grape vine and the pair of them were blocking the steps up to her balcony. There will be no grapes as she had some crazy idea that to prune after mid-March would make the vine bleed to death so it got left. Do I care? Actually not at all, I have finished with that garden and with S as its owner. Everything has turned out as I told her it would if certain things were not carried out, such as a ton or so of horse manure, deep mulching, watering, cutting off surplus branches to let in light and air, and more. She does not deserve her garden. I spoke to MGF about this only yesterday, suggesting that he might like to return there and continue what he now so long ago began.

'No! I have finished, *finished* with that!' he said most emphatically, slicing the air as if for a karate neck-break. 'She has got young B working for her at the moment, I do not suppose he knows a great deal but his father has a good garden, perhaps it will be okay. But as for me . . .'

'Finished? Like me?' He nodded, and we both felt comforted and vindicated. S's karma is at work; long as she might for Paradise on Earth, she will have to humble her proud spirit and learn about the plants she professes to love, and also, she will have to truly get into contact with the earth instead of simply wandering over it with her feet bare, making noises of ecstasy in spring.

MGF came out to look at my garden. Nothing escaped his notice. To fill in where a petunia had given up the ghost I had placed what appeared to be a multicoloured godetia, a plant which perhaps surprisingly I had never seen before.

'There's three there. They are annuals. Related to evening primrose, clarkia.'

'Oneagraceae!' I rattled off proudly and he nodded, not acknowledging my achievement of memory.

'You can sow them outdoors in spring, you don't need to buy them at a garden centre.'

'But I should then either have too many or none, you know I don't have room here to scatter a whole packet.'

He shrugged. We looked at the stem of the godetia. It certainly did look like a single plant, with three shades of flower growing on it. He said nothing. Could he be wrong? Could there be such a phenomenal thing as a plant with three colours of flower on it?

He approved of my begonias, he laughed admiringly at my Edna Everage display of gladdies. He approved of my having recently replanted one of my largest alpine bowls, leaving out the bulbs the leaves of which keep off the light from small plants in spring. He it was who advised me that bulbs and alpines together in troughs are a bad idea. Iris leaves take months to wither and look awful. He was impressed with my second flowering of roses. He made my day by noticing a small fern which I have been watching double and double again in size, growing in the lovely clay pot which D gave me not long before she died. It is a *Dryopteris sieboldii* and may well grow to a height of a metre in time. Nobody else has noticed it, or the fact that a polypodium and some violets and *Ajuga reptans* are now filling up the old sink, growing down in the dark, to my intense joy. We discussed the possible renewal of my old tub, which contains the Patagonian/Irish type of fuchsia, and possibly the old root of the sumac, and a clump of *Iris foetidissima* and some Sweet Williams (*Dianthus barbatus*) and an enormous scarlet begonia.

I have an idea forming in my mind these past weeks that I could well sacrifice all these and plant one of the new very dark red-leaved acers, those with multiple cut-leaves, intensely graceful. I worry that it would not have enough light underneath the high arching roses. I have just pruned a half dozen huge branches off the fuchsia to allow light to get into the far corner and give it a chance with what water is available to it; to my great delight, MGF thought this a splendid plan, so I shall be looking out for the perfect specimen in the near future. I have one worry though, which is that the beautiful dark leaves will not look well against the dark old brick wall. MGF says it will thrive in such a sheltered spot because even though it is a north-facing wall, light now falls there in the late afternoon. And why? Did MGF notice why? He did not.

That poor old cousin of the acer, the vile sycamore has gone! Cut down in its prime, rooted out. My garden is filled with the light and sun which is its natural right again. I thanked the neighbour profusely. My kitchen is lighter too. Almost, in this very hot summer, I almost long for its shade but dare not even think such a thing. That would be perversity.

But how to create the right background for an acer? I cannot paint the wall cream, it is not possible to get the brush behind the rose branches and the ivy. I have an inspiration.

I am going to fix a large mirror on the wall behind the tub, and have the illusion of two acers and a double view of the brilliant gladdies and the agapanthus and sweet peas directly opposite.

My rabbit hole garden is to expand ever more, mirrors everywhere. And what shall be the fairest of them all? The Japanese maple or acer, somewhat bonsai in its tub, sheltered but with light all around it so that it shall not grow twisted.

I think I shall visit some nurseries tomorrow, and ring up a couple of people to see if they would care for donations of the contents of the tub. I think the ex-soldier son might benefit from a wild sort of hardy fuchsia, his pretty wife is Irish and it will remind her of home, where they fill the hedges. It will grow quite large and flower grandly, create a mite of shade enough for the irises and maybe a fern or so. Will they appreciate this new arrangement? I think so, for they are now aiming not so much to create a corner of a municipal park as a proper garden, with surprises and secrecy and little miracles which other people do not notice. Which is, after all, part of the point of a garden. Every garden is its own secret society.

And at the foot of the acer, nothing but woodchips or cocoshell? Very probably, but now wouldn't this be the perfect spot for either cyclamen or colchicums, perhaps both, one in spring and one in autumn? Excitement surges again, and I realise for the hundredth time that even in a tiny space you can continue to create and recreate infinitely. There is no such thing as an instant garden, which is finally *done*. And every time you have the visitor, you can have something new to show. Eventually they begin to see things for themselves and then you will have real joy.

14

The Plagues of Egypt

We all have days when everything seems to go against us. Gardeners sometimes suffer from weeks on end of such days. That there are not more suicides amongst gardeners is a monument to our mental and spiritual stamina, as well as the excellence of our philosophic stance. We enjoy a challenge.

Which can only be right, as there are plenty of challenges, especially to the uninitiated. Your new plants are like children, and, even if this way of putting a fact makes you wince, it is still true. Hence the term 'nursery'. So it strikes panic and dismay into the stoutest heart when horrible yellow patches, black spots, unidentified insects, slime, webs, weird fluff and mysterious white powders appear on what were marvellous plants only hours ago. Why me? you shout at the sky, hair and eyes wild, voice loud with grief. Why indeed?

Aphids are probably the most ubiquitous and iniquitous life-form on earth – or so I said last year when all my honeysuckle was sucked to crinkle-crisps, a flowerless blackened mass of rope. This was because I had not taken my reading-glasses down the garden path, and my magnifying glass, and had not noticed the things until it was too late. By then they had done not only the above described harm, but spread to other plants, taking with them some incurable plant AIDS, an unknown virus which twisted leaves everywhere. I could have wept but I was in shock. The misery which clutched my heart could hardly have been excelled if I had been diagnosed as HIV positive, in fact I could have coped with that more bravely. I would have kept jolly quiet about it for a start, whereas dead and dying plants are a screeching announcement of shame. Clearly, I had been practising unsafe gardening. But when you get to know a few facts about aphids, as with AIDS, being attacked is not shaming. Anybody can get it, like the common cold.

My daughter the ecologist tells me that aphids reproduce both parthenogenetically, and occasionally by sexual means, in order to strengthen the gene-pool. They are also – think of this – born pregnant, which speeds up their reproductive rate to fast forward. If all the predators which help to control aphids disappeared, then within one year there would be enough aphids to cover the entire surface of the earth to a depth of two metres. Aphids can detect the kind of plant they wish to feed upon from – how high up was it, a mile, a hundred metres? – from an uncannily huge distance. They are known as the plant louse, greenfly (I think this includes blackfly and some of the young ones are pink), homoptera, and ant-cows. This last is because sometimes ants will herd greenfly and stroke them in order to milk them. Therefore, the ant also becomes our enemy. What safely kills ants? Am I to keep an ant-eater in my little rabbit hole garden? Shall it include not only Hidcote, Kiftsgate, Upton, Sezincote and Biddulph Grange, but the fauna of the

Yucatan? It would certainly be original, most people go no further than frogs, tortoises and hedgehogs.

We have in the aphid an enemy to be reckoned with. And worse, if we do away with them altogether in our own patch by intensive spraying then the ladybirds, for example, will disappear as well, and then the aphids will return in doubled (quadrupled and more) force without anything to eat them up. To think of this makes me feel the need to go and lie down, take to some serious drinking or go dormant like a snail, sealed in my shell until the rains come. And, that sticky stuff which exudes onto whatever is under an aphid-infested branch is aphid faeces. Yuck, bleaaggh. If you have nasturtiums without blackfly, roses without greenfly, you have miracles. Or you have been spraying too much and will be punished. The best way is to examine plants closely in early March and spray judiciously, not indulging in overkill techniques just to be on the safe side. If you wash aphids off with soapy water all will seem to be well for a while, but they climb back up the plants after their shower.

Never kill a ladybird, although they can seem like a plague in themselves at times. Was it 1975 when we were cursed with them? biting our skin even, teeming millions wherever you went. They were so numerous in Staffordshire that one could not avoid treading on them, all over the pavements, everything tinged with scarlet. Didn't like that at all although we did not purposely kill them, just brushed them off our hair and skin, reciting 'Fly away home' like a mantra.

When I was a child I was terrified of anything which crept, crawled and flew. I have already related how strands of cotton could produce paranoia in an impressionable child. This terror had been instilled into me by my mother's operant conditioning. She had terminal entomoarachnophobia. She used to suck spiders up the vacuum cleaner and if they came into the bath she would scald them with boiling water. I remember one which returned up the plughole seven times to be scalded yet again as this torturer my mother laughed with delighted glee. I was five at the time so can hardly be blamed for laughing too. A favourite game of mine one summer was to sit in the field playing with columns of ants by mixing up mud to build walls across their path, making them turn where I willed. That lots got buried in the process is now a cause for shame, but I had not been taught respect for life. Rather the opposite. I am just intensely grateful that generally speaking my sadistic side is very weak. She used to hit spiders with a crepe-soled shoe if they crawled across the bedroom wall. We had lots of them because the bungalow was perched on top of an ancient ivy-covered mill set into a small cliff in some woodland. Spiders like ivy. Last night there was the largest spider in the universe on my bedroom floor. I did nothing. Downstairs in the parlour another, even bigger, walked across the floor to hide under the table. I did nothing. You can overcome your childhood, and it doesn't wash to blame your parents for your own shortcomings. Forty-legs were another of her more extreme hatreds as were earwigs and woodlice. Earwigs frighten a lot of people, and only in recent years can I tolerate them near me. In fact, since I really became obsessed with gardening, my fear of things which creepeth upon the earth has lessened, not increased. You cannot kill everything, all that death and the impulse to decimate cancels out all the good feeling of watching plants thrive and grow. There has to be balance somewhere.

Now, I welcome all spiders both in the garden and in the house, just so long as they do not try to get into bed with me. Spiders are good, and I hate the thought of them being killed. Only a few years ago I was very nervous of them running into my hair as I pruned bushes, or up my sleeves or down my neck if I barged into a web by mistake. Now, it simply doesn't matter. They run so fast they are off you and back into the plants before you have time to work up a decent fit of hysterics. Of course, if this was Australia I might feel very differently because of the death dealing funnel-web. In fact, in Australia, I could not contemplate gardening. Allowing a funnel-web to run up my arm is going just too far, even if I became a fully fledged Buddhist. However, if the climatic change towards heat continues, soon the funnel-webs will be with us, having travelled for free on aeroplanes. Meanwhile, plant pests are my greatest terror, in case they harm the plants. I get palpitations every time I see an alien creature standing nonchalantly on one of my leaves. I am learning a lot about the creepy-crawly world and find it fascinating. Ways to keep plants alive and healthy without creating worse problems are what we must look for whenever possible.

I had a patch of eau-de-cologne mint one year, a delightful but galloping plant. It was suddenly covered in small iridescent green beetles, so many of them that it shimmered like metal in the sun. These I considered a blessing, something to show to people, none of whom had ever seen the like. Then they disappeared, and the eau-de-cologne mint disappeared as well. Nothing else. I may never know what happened there, it is simply an enigma, of no great importance as it happens. In a rabbit hole there really is no room for things which spread rapidly. And I often found cute little beetles simply clinging to walls and leaves both indoors and out. They were very slow-moving things and did not appear to do much harm, so I kindly left them alone. Meanwhile I was losing some of the plants in pots, and numerous holes appeared in the leaves of some plants, notably a *Hydrangea petiolaris* which looked quite ugly and unwell.

'Look at these things,' I said to MGF one day. 'I've never seen anything like this, what do you think they are?' He burst out laughing, a scornful whine with the note of triumph in it which I find difficult to understand. It reminds me of those children in playgrounds who mock the unfortunate, those wearing handed-down clothes, those with greying shirts, those who wet their knickers when the nitnurse comes.

'Adult vine weevils! You've got vine weevils, God, you'll never get rid of them, you'll have to root everything out and burn it.' Well, I know how to deal with bullies. You do not let them see that you are perturbed.

'Oh, surely that's too drastic, there must be some way to control them.' He picked one off a dahlia flower, dropped it on the path and trod on it.

182

'And even then, if you kill all these, they are not the worst of it. It is the larvae of these beetles which live in the soil and eat away at roots. I shouldn't be surprised if it wasn't them which killed off all your pansies.'

'I thought you said that was pansy sickness. What is that, anyway?'

'Nobody knows. Perhaps you've got both. But these will eat off the roots and then of course the plant dies.'

'Well I suppose I'll have to change the compost in some of the pots.'

'All the pots I should think.' I said no more, but did some research. There is a powder containing a chemical called BHC which used to be called HCH, according to Collins Guide to Pests and Diseases, and on the pack it also uses the word 'lindane'. I am not at all sure that this stuff should be legal, and must be used with great caution. I decided first of all to try an ecological method. You can now buy packs of a culture of annelids which eat vine weevil larvae. The method is rather expensive but not as costly and troublesome as clearing out around seventy-five pots. I got some, used it carefully according to instructions, and apparently it worked. Except in one large pot. Why? I could perhaps have missed this pot when watering on the precious annelid soup. It was my acid soil pot. The camellia bloomed once at Christmas and then turned down. MGF told me it was frost, but other plants in this large pot were suffering. I was watering it with specially collected rainwater, got by cutting a hole in the edge of the lid of an ancient huge nappy bucket and inserting the last section of drainpipe through this. On a rainy day the bucket was soon filled. The water therein did look rather strange, but I paid no attention to this at first, I just watered the acid tub with it, feeling very clever. The water turned first brown, then black. I cleaned it all out and began again. This time I could see a film which looked like oil or petrol on the surface of the water. This I tried to avoid when watering. I could not think where it was coming from, and mentioned it to the all-knowing MGF.

'Well you know, aeroplanes unload surplus fuel into the atmosphere before landing, they simply spray it all over us, and I reckon it is thick on your roof and the rain is washing it into your bucket.' There was a terrible logic and an aura of revealed truth about this. Had I been of a political frame of mind I would have found myself petitioning door-to-door about this, and also the other fact which MGF told me, which is that aeroplane toilets spray out their contents, viruses, bacteria and everything. Sometimes it descends frozen. It is theoretically possible to be hit on the head by a lump of frozen faeces, a humiliating event at best. In this modern world we are inundated with our own sewage from all sides. Anyway, it would seem that the petrol killed my camellia, a lithospermum, and two gentians. But, when I began to rake out this tragic little graveyard, I also found two vine weevil larvae. Therefore, when refilling the tub I shook in a very little of that lindane powder, feeling nervous and guilty because it seems so violent.

And last week I found two adult vine weevils in a dahlia flower which I had brought into the house in order to paint it. The home-made water butt has been ditched, acid-loving plants are ruled out now, and perhaps it is time to get another pack of the annelid soup. But vine weevils are sneaky and nasty. I have a delightful crassula, which I almost lost, which would have been very sad because D gave it to me from a large clump which I admired. It is a fleshy rosette with glaucous blueish leaves. I also had a sempervivum which would have grown very large, except it kept jumping out of its pot. Every morning there it was on the floor, I could not understand it. Investigation revealed a vine weevil larva right in its heart, which I ditched but it was too late. The sempervivum leapt out finally to its death, a strange phenomenon which I cannot explain. I do not think a larva less than two centimetres long would have the strength. Did my cat Emma knock it out of its pot at night, and if so why that and not others? This kind of rock plant is very susceptible to vine weevils, so if yours begin to fail, unpot them and scrape out any offending creatures, put them into new compost and all shall be well. Cute little beetles? Sadly, no.

Snails have already been mentioned. They can, in warmish rainy weather, be so numerous that you begin to get the heeby-jeebies in a small space. Removing them to the wild may seem kind but is not, as MGF pointed out to me. If you reduce the numbers of adults to too few then more hatch out to make up the numbers. Carefully placed pellets and a lot of hunting are the best method. In a rabbit hole you cannot afford to let them chomp and rasp their way through all your best plants. Patricia Highsmith loved snails and kept them as pets, but she also wrote a story about being eaten alive by snails. Nasty.

Helix aspersa. (Beady gut)

I have a special snail-spoon. This is an old silver tablespoon with which I scoop them up and then, aiming carefully, I hurl them some fifty or more metres into the churchyard across the alley. God will take care of their souls, or perhaps a Roman god. I could win a silver Olympic medal for snail-hurling, I really put some bicep into this process. Some day I expect to hear a roar of rage as somebody in the usually deserted yard catches a snail down their collar, and to have it hurled right back, but as this is usually a night raid the risk is small. MGF tells me that the best way to be rid of too many snails is to step on them, or use a large hammer. I am ashamed to say that I am too squeamish to do this, death must take place out of my sight. But this year none of this has been necessary. As with my gypsy method of keeping ants out of the house, I did actually try something similar with the snails. I had a serious talk with them, and I have only seen one since. I am thinking of setting up as a garden pest control mystic. Of course, it could have something to do with the baking weather, and the fact that they are all sealed up in their shells dreaming of autumn downpours.

Orange slugs are rather horrible, and some years quite a lot appear, and then not again for a long time. The year these strange molluscs marauded my patch was the last in which I cooked one of my favourite dishes: *moules marinière*, which I have modified to include turmeric and *nori*, or sometimes *arame*, two types of a Japanese seaweed, which makes a really wonderful dish. Not any more I fear, because once I had noticed how closely the orange slug and the mussel resemble one another, I was finished. The enormous black slug is apparently beneficial. It is a carnivore, and will happily eat other slugs. So if you can bear them, leave them alone, they are our friends.

I do not know what nips the buds off some of my sweet peas; MGF says it 'an insect' which nibbles through the stalk, but this I find rather vague. I suspect birds of swooping down and pinching them, and this I can tolerate. I like it when birds appear, but if I had an allotment I might have to resort to netting for raspberries and peas. As it is, I am sentimental about birds, which are more frequent since Emma became too old to hunt. I think I have a nest in the clematis outside my bedroom window, which is wonderful even if they do scream at dawn, and one day I was privileged with a bird visitor which was certainly not a pest.

I was sitting contemplating the arrangement of ferns opposite my bench when I heard a terrific commotion in the churchyard, like an angered cat screaming. Then something flew very fast over my head, made another commotion as it disentangled itself from the *montana* and then flew fast again, to rest on the top of my antique carved clothes-post. I could not believe my eyes. There perched a large hawk, surveying the territory all around. It stayed there for some minutes, perhaps recovering its dignity after failing to catch a cat for lunch, or perhaps a rat, I shall never know. And then it wheeled rapidly off, climbing higher in the town sky to become an exciting memory.

The pest problem is more intense in small spaces with lots of walls, pots and crannies for creatures to hide in, and any diseases spread very quickly because everything touches something else, and a disease-bearing aphid does not have far to go with its infections. You have to inspect often, and act fast, or you risk losing everything.

This year I raised some small trailing petunias which I planned to drape out of pots, off the roof and a hanging basket. I managed to harden them off and risked putting them out early, with success. MGF said that he would concede that although these plants were vulgar, he actually would like one, as the flowers on the purple rose variety were exactly like a larger version of his favourite geranium. We went to the garden centre, he pretending that he was not really there, only to find a prominent notice informing us that this year all petunias (and tomatoes) had been affected by virus. We thought, probably tobacco mosiac. The assistant told us gloomily that simply touching an infected plant and then another plant is enough to spread the disease. MGF was disappointed, but rather unsympathetic when my plants were apparently affected. Two of them seem to have recovered, and I think that the intense heat and sudden extra sunlight when the offending sycamore was cut down may be the reason most of the leaves turned yellow. But for a while I was in a panic, and very careful about not going over all the plants at once without washing my hands. I felt like typhoid Mary.

Then you have to see that a very small garden is a microcosm of how life works; life, death, life, death, in continuing cycles, taking all events as part of itself. To become too distressed over losses is a kind of greed just as too great a delight over abundance is not only greedy, but tempting fate. And every year in the garden is different. MGF names years in the garden as The Year of the Snail or The Year of the Late Frost. I hope he never has to see my garden in distress and say 'Well of course darling, its the Year of the Flatworm.' Uurrgh! These things really spook me, they are the most recent curse and affliction, about which nothing can yet be done.

They are New Zealand flatworms, and as we may all have seen on television, they wind themselves around dear old earthworms and strangle them. I have, by the way, recently acquired a television set in order to find out if I was missing anything. I was missing some excellent gardening programmes, some scientific programmes which for my taste could be more detailed and thorough but are not without interest, and some excellent humour, and the terrible news of flatworms. These, seen close up on screen, were more frightening than even the most disgusting Stephen King. I knew about flatworms before, in another context. During the Sixties and early Seventies, scientists had a great argument going, and perhaps still have, about flatworms. There was a magazine called The Worm Runners Digest. The theory being tested was whether it might be possible for memory to be transmitted in cells by eating them. I wrote a science fiction story around that time in which a wicked scientist ate the brain of a good and exceedingly clever scientist to get all her knowledge and power. Cannibals believed that to eat the brain of an enemy was to take in his power. There was a ghastly denouement and punishment for this un-scientific behaviour, of course, but meanwhile the worm runners were teaching flatworms how to run up and down certain patterns in order to be rewarded with food, then chopping them up and feeding them to untrained flatworms. These well-fed cannibal flatworms could then perform the tasks without being trained. That is QED as far as I am concerned, but scientists are notoriously hard to convince. I rather think that the flatworms they used for these experiments were a small kind, but the flatworms which are now infesting our British gardens are a few inches long, with a mottled topside and a horrible whitish underbelly. They can slither through in-credibly small spaces, disappearing under stones and have even been known to escape from closed screw-top jars. The Houdini of the pest world, you can't keep them either in or out! And in any numbers, they will ruin our soil because without earthworms our soil will become dust. To date, no working cure has been found, although research continues briskly. They prefer acid soil, but arrive anywhere from an inadvertently infested nursery in the soil of migrant plants. For a while I was in nightmare city about these creatures, thinking how devastated I would be if everything was slowly laid to waste with no recourse or revenge. I have not found one flatworm yet. Apart from this bit of text, I simply refuse to think about it. After all, my earthworms are rather special, and not very many at that.

When I first began to cultivate this tiny amount of earth I noticed no worms. MGF dug some up out of S's garden, and we put them into mine, where they seem to be fairly at home although still not numerous. Earthworms are totally beneficial. These are another life form which used to terrify me as a child, and I still do not really care to handle them, but I love them dearly and am always glad when one appears. Could we rid ourselves of flatworms by cutting them up and feeding them to other flatworms I wonder? We would probably get a race of giant and super intelligent beasts and be very sorry for interfering. There has to be something which will see them off, we must hope hard.

Another plague is a hailstorm. It will beat the petals off flowers in a few minutes, and there is nothing to be done about it, you can't go running around with umbrellas, you just have to watch mournfully from indoors. It is all part of working in with the scheme of things, after all, grumbling and moaning is part of being a gardener. There is always either too much rain or too little, and when it rains it rains petrol, which is hardly any better than blood or frogs, as in the Fortean publications. Frogs would be welcome. Locusts not.

The truth is that a garden is not a natural phenomenon at all, that by creating it you have created an unbalanced and utterly artificial situation, and must expect repercussions. 'Wild garden', may I say this again, is a contradiction in terms, a risible concept not properly thought through. Cultivation is something which is effected upon natural life forms, not the reverse. The object of gardening is to produce a place in which valuable experiences can happen, without any real damage having taken place. This means moderation and being tolerant of a few losses, and learning more and more about the intricate controls which creatures exert upon one another, including the gardener with a few carefully chosen poisons used very judiciously. Poor S, with her completely 'natural' garden has no vegetables and few flowers, which is a shame when it was so nearly a wonderful achievement. I wonder how her new slave is faring? Has he wept at the far end of the tangled Shrine Walk yet, ears burning from being told off for doing exactly as he was told? Neither MGF nor I care about that any more.

Drought. Hosepipe bans. Terror. Are we to stand by and watch our beloved creations slowly die because the water company keep all the money for themselves and allow water to dribble away? What happened to all the winter rain, did they not hoard it? Well, take heart, because too much watering is not good for a garden. Hosepipe water has chlorine in it for a start, you can get sappy weak stems from overwatering, but shallow root systems. How to use as little water as possible?

First of all, anyone lucky enough to have a big lawn should seriously consider its sacrifice. A lawn must be the least ecologically sound planting arrangement in any garden where water is not plentiful, certainly not very Green in a drought. This climate is no longer suitable for lawns, which to be green must be sprinkled continually in hot weather, and that really must be a waste. Have paved and pebbled paths and patios in between beds and borders, and keep the soil not only well covered in plants, but mulched thickly over a good soaking. This cuts down watering to very little, and strengthens a lot of plants which will put down deeper roots to find deeper layers of water. I feel very superior, here in my little world, with no lawn. Should I ever acquire a larger patch, I shall have no lawn. No sprinkling, no artificial fertilisers, no selective weedkiller, no electric lawnmower using up power and disturbing the neighbours, no noisy children playing football. I shall have a series of small enclosed gardens instead, each one completely different from the last. And I shall mulch deeply.

I have recently mulched every bare inch of soil or compost with coco shell, which is delightful stuff to use as it smells richly of chocolate, and by the time I had used 120 litres I was almost giggling, I felt quite high on the fumes. The stuff really does keep the water from evaporating. You will need to poke down through it to test the soil with a finger from time to time, and it usually contacts moist soil, which is very gratifying when the temperature is above 32 °C. A drought need not be a plague in a garden; you may lose a plant or so, but not even that if you can lift pails of used water out from the house when things get really desperate. And no moles will ruin your lawn if you do not have one, eliminating the need for harming them. Not having a lawn will release you so that you have time and enthusiasm to do some real gardening. I look back on all those hours I spent perfecting lawns in the past as a time of complete error, an unthinking copying of a fashion which in the first place arose, not for visual effect, but for the drying of linen (lawn). The more I think about it, the lawn itself is a plague. Fruit bushes would be better, and more delicious.

Perhaps though, your lawn is your pet, and you could not bear to have it killed off just like that. In which case, I sympathise. I have a pet plant. It is an ophiopogon, which I fell extravagantly in love with when I first saw it, I think at Sherbourne but it may have been Hidcote. They, like many once-unusual plants, can be got easily now, but a few years ago I had to consult MGF who consulted his MGF who was fully qualified in horticulture, who knew of a nursery where . . . and in due course it arrived. I was so proud of it and planted it in my best blue ceramic container with some small blue irises underneath and a bit of *Sedum spathulifolium*, which I felt would look wonderful. I mulched it all with grit, and was well pleased. A couple of years went by, and then I got small purple flowers, the irises came and went, the sedum spread, and then so did the ophiopogon. Like the spider plant, which I think may be a relative, it bore tufty children, one or two of which I dared to transplant into the edge of the narrow bed, recalling MGF saying that it made a nice border. I could visualise a lush black fringe all along the edge, with orange crocus behind it in spring. These transplants promptly died. Then the main plant started to look rather withered, which to me means more water. It got worse. I needed a specialist.

'Oh you've overwatered it, it's probably rotten underneath,' said MGF spitefully. I was killing it with kindness, my favourite, my most decorative conversation piece. Not one visitor had failed to notice it and ask what it was, giving me the chance to rattle off its lovely name, and to explain that it was not a black grass, nor a clown's wig, but a member of the liliacea. I repotted it and did not overwater it but things got no better. During the Great Vine Weevil Scare I took it out again only to find, not a larva but a small red worm, right at its heart. Could this be yet another pest? I got rid of it, repotted what was left of the plant and waited. For a year now, there has been a bit of dried black stuff in a pot, and I am unwilling to admit that it is dead, and chuck it out. Any moment now it will spring to life with glossy new spears like strips shaved off a kitchen range.

If you feel as tenderly about your lawn as I feel about my ophiopogon, then I sympathise. I shall feel traitorous simply going out to buy a new one.

Or shall I? Actually not, I think I shall go later this afternoon and pretend that the whole sad saga never happened. But first I must inspect the present plant; perhaps it isn't officially dead after all?

195

And the other destructive force for gardens, especially in an enclosed space, is the wind. Everything grows taller than usual down a rabbit hole, trying to get its share of the light. Wind, when it strikes, creates a whirling in a back yard enclosed by walls, and is stronger than if you had tall plants in the centre of an open space, where some of the force blows through stems. Many plants dislike strong wind because it dries them out, scorching the leaves, and the coldness of wind harms a lot of plants too. And of course they can be broken. You must support everything if you do not want it destroyed, but in a small space too many canes are ugly and dangerous. When my grandson was very young I was terrified in case he should fall on a cane and hurt an eye, so I got some of those jolly rubber toppers, a very pleasing solution. But now I have discovered something even better.

Y-stakes have been invented, and I discovered these through the Hardy Plant Society. They come in various heights, are just about invisible, and have bendy arms which lovingly support plants, keeping them from lying on the path. Droopy fuchsias and shy giant begonias look much better with a Y-stake under them, and you can actually see the magnificent pendulous faces of my enormous white and orange begonias, and the flowers do not drop off as quickly. I am like a child with a new set of toys, and want to add to my collection as if it was Lego. I recall feeling like that with my first vine-eyes, and my first woolly basket-liner. Yet another aspect of garden happiness, plagues notwithstanding.

15

Further Initiations

There came the day when my knowledge of gardening, incomplete as it was and always will be, was nevertheless strong enough for me to occasionally offer advice. I had for some time been stretching my luck and my muscles by arguing with MGF, and become the proud owner of a few grudging concessions that yes, I was right, or possibly right under certain circumstances. I was shown selected texts from MGF's large collection of plant books, lent them sometimes against my will ('but I am writing/ painting/in the middle of reading something else, I simply can't . . .'), always finding myself reading and having to discuss what he wanted. MGF has many weaknesses but he shows remarkable powers when making other people do what he wants. He should have been a professional teacher.

I am sometimes consulted on garden visits when I go with another 'J' and G, two teachers of art who are both creating new gardens. Neither of them had much knowledge of the subject, so where possible I offer what I know. This is a pleasing thing to do but also a bit frightening. I do not want to be blamed for gardening which goes wrong. We three have many similar interests and passions, and the need to create a garden is just one of them. This certainly seems to create excellent communications and shared jokes and enthusiasms. Both these men seem to have green fingers. (I wonder why Americans call a feeling for raising plants a green thumb? Strange people.)

In a few days' time it is likely that I shall be taking them for a day out, one of several we have already undertaken and plan for the future. It is one of life's greatest pleasures assisting other people to buy good examples of the right plants. I plan for Batsford in the morning, and then in the afternoon, the especial pleasure of Sezincote. MGF first showed me Sezincote, and such a special trip that was, although only one of several itineraries he had planned, all of which taught me something as well as being a source of pleasure. He made me buy a copy of the Yellow Book, and off we went to Blockley Gardens. Sometimes there are several private gardens to visit on one designated day in a village, and Blockley is rather special.

The Yellow Book is obtainable annually from bookshops and contains a list of all the gardens in the National Garden Society, which at certain times are open to the public. Instructions for getting there, information about what kind of garden to expect, and so on are all included, and it is the key to beautiful summers. The Good Gardens Guide is even more comprehensive. Usually the gardens are not crowded with people, and always they are fascinating. Blockley does not sound interesting but it is a really desirable Cotswold village just up the road from Batsford, where the Miftford girls hid in the linen cupboards to keep warm during their childhood. MGF had not been to Blockley for some long time, so it was a day of discovery for him too as it turned out. Again, we went in blazing sunshine, the kind of day which Laurie Lee's childhood took place in, echoing blue sky, buzzing green hedges, rural heaven. I would not have marvelled if the elderly ladies at the cottage doors wore crossover print aprons and had put their fruit pies on the windowsills to cool. More likely they were all in their back gardens in bikinis swilling cocktails, freezer still full of last year's pies. Blockley was very quiet. I held my breath as we found a place to park, and we made a tour plan. Some of the gardens, needless to say, were much better than others, but this is always a matter of opinion and taste. Every one was very worth a visit.

Blockley appears to be built in a deep rift on a series of shelves, which makes most of the gardens very steep, and offers opportunity for some interesting landscaping. Some of the small stone terrace-houses had a good length of garden in front, built up behind strong stone walls with steps behind iron gates. This is a style which reminded me strongly of parts of Halifax, excepting that in my childhood all the stone was black, and I grew up thinking that grass was sooty in its nature. If history had been slightly different, and Leeds not so near to a source of coal, the great woollen mills would have filled the Cotswolds after the Industrial Revolution. The woollen mills up north are now theatres, art centres, antique galleries and the kind of restaurant which gets a page in the Sunday *Observer*. Halifax and Hebden Bridge are now quite as tourist orientated as the Cotswolds. Someday the whole of these islands will be a great theme park for visiting aliens. MGF and I felt a bit like that at first, Blockley was like a ghost town. But then we located the yellow signs which indicate where to start the garden tours. You pay a small fee and are marked with a yellow sticker. People began to appear, in modern dress.

I had not been there half an hour when I was wondering if there was an estate agent so I could check out prices. I knew it would be beyond me, of course, the meanest hovel in the Cotswolds costs a lot of money, which is beginning to be the case up north too. Everyone with any talent of my generation got away from there as soon as possible, and now we can't afford to go back, it is full of artists and writers from down south.

We enjoyed some of these very steep gardens, discussing the cleverness of the owners in getting groups of plants level with the back upstairs windows. There were plenty of flowers, and I lusted after impossibilities, as I always do, such as kniphofia, which would never do well in my small space. There are quite a few varieties of this plant besides the usual 'red-hot poker', and I love them because they look so very exotic, like flowering cacti. I visualise a circular bed in some huge garden filled entirely with various kniphofia, flowering yuccas and a few *Lobelia cardinalis*. Rather 'public park', but it would look splendid. For about six weeks a year. Even quite ordinary houses, with gardens not in the tour, had marvellous clumps of flowers which I think of as difficult, such as gazanias and gerberas and rudbeckia, everything looking very healthy.

And then we went to Joanna Southcott's house.

We were both struck at once with an atmosphere of something very special. The whole house and garden are built into what is almost a cliff, with a short steep drive which then snakes slowly up and up. There is a terrace at the back of the house with a most interesting view, from a balcony which feels like being on board a tall ship. And then you go up again, into what gradually becomes a stretch of woodland, which levels off to high fields. It is a like an enchanted place. I thought of my tiny garden and felt that it was so ordinary, so conventional, so banal. I longed to live there, in Joanna Southcott's house, which had a solid mysterious style, Cotswold stone subtly aged, huge pointed wooden shutters on all the windows. It was somehow Germanic, and dark, and secret. You longed to go inside. Then we realised that in fact this was an extensive garden without any flowers at all. No attempt at all had been made to 'brighten it up', but rather the opposite. Wonderful! True style! The complete antithesis of my rather crammed effect. It was well filled with shrubs, and although spacious had an air of intimacy, every turn in the path had secrets. MGF had a look of ecstasy on his face and for a brief moment I wondered if he had received an Annunciation, but the glazed eyes denoted appreciation and pleasure.

He began redesigning S's garden, ripping out all her flowers and bringing in more shrubs and hedges. Her roses would of course be the very first to go. He asked me who Joanna Southcott was, anyway; had she designed the garden?

I knew nothing of that, but thought probably not; I told him what I recalled about Joanna which was not a great deal. Phantom pregnancy in a woman with Messianic delusions provided us with some subdued merriment for a while, and MGF wanted to know why they did not simply open the box to find out what was in it. Probably better kept shut, like Pandora's I told him. It was a very long time since I had read a book on this arcane history, but I think I recalled that the religious group were based elsewhere at the time she went into labour. No matter, this would have been the perfect setting. We realised to our surprise that for once we were more interested in the landscaping than the plants. I had a flash of inspiration in which I built steps up onto the outhouse roof, with alpines at the edges, but quickly abandoned it as my silliest idea that year. Might as well leave the house key outside on a labelled hook.

One of the owners of this house was sitting out on his lower terrace and we exchanged a few pleasantries. We offered some compliments, trying not to gush hopelessly, and we could see that this rather handsome man was pleased. We had another walk around the very difficult pathways, and I tried to analyse just what it was which was so attractive about this place.

There were a few pleasant scents, and indeed we did finally find one or two shrubs with insignificant flowers, but over all this wonderful atmosphere. Was there some religious or mystical aura about this very splendid dwelling and its surroundings? Were we so thrilled not only with the style of the place, but because Ms Southcott herself, if only in our imaginations, had stumbled wearily up these paths, lightly *enceinte*, leaving a trail of meaning behind for sensitive souls such as us? No, not really; what we sensed was the aura of a very great deal of solid money. It is irresistibly magnetic, and especially attractive when it is not ostentatiously displayed. We just knew that here they *could* have as many exotic flowers as they liked, plus an enormous conservatory, ponds, fountains, everything, but had chosen not. Feeling spiritually elevated, we bid a restrained goodbye and floated off to the next garden on the list.

It is possible that it was during this strolling from garden to garden that I was also possessed by something little more than an idle daydream, but which nags away at me from time to time. How marvellous it would be to be in the NGS handbook, and be the hostess in a very interesting and pleasant garden, undoubtedly their smallest. There are surprisingly no other gardens in Leamington in their pages, and this is not because town gardens do not feature, for there are several in Birmingham for example. The prospect is both enchanting and terrifying. I would have to choose a date for the publication, and then make damn sure that all was perfect. And how can you ever do that in any garden? If you have a large garden then it is excusable and even expected that something will have failed; this only serves to show that everything else is successful. A visitor could walk a hundred yards away from some disaster area and see so many pleasant things in that space that any failure would be forgotten. Even so, visitors sometimes think that everything should be leaf-perfect; MGF and I overheard a few spiteful complaints about lupin seeds and slug damage from silly people who obviously did not garden themselves and, therefore, did not know the difficulties of getting everything into perfect condition at the same time.

In a tiny space like mine, every leaf is significant. I go round every day nipping off anything which is not healthy or fresh, I dead-head continually, turn pots this way and that to get the best effect, and still there will be something glaring at me. Only yesterday I found I had yellowing leaves on my Grenadier. And what if today were Visiting Day? I look very closely and can find no cause although there could just be red spider mite under those leaves. A leaf-cutter bee has been busy on the rose just outside the french window, lacy leaves seem very prominent in such a place. This year of drought is not the best for trailing petunias and the *Clematis viticella* is finally over. I could not show this place off to anyone who was expecting Chelsea Flower Show in a teacup, there would be disappointment and humiliation. But what a lovely daydream all the same. Three visitors at one time would be the maximum, tea would be served in my best china, and questions and compliments would fly back and forth at a heady pace. I might even make cakes and scones to sell for charity, which is the point of the NGS open days, and have little pots to sell with seedlings and cuttings from something very difficult to rear.

No harm in dreaming.

There were half a dozen gardens open that day, and we saw them all, but the most remarkable, by which I mean those causing the greatest number of remarks from MGF and not a few from me, was also the largest. Neither of us had ever seen anything quite like this. It was undoubtedly the garden with everything. For a start it had a large pond with an island, with a little bridge across for the ducks which waddled obligingly back and forth as if they could not swim. This island reminded me of the one in the Graham Greene short story, rather sinister as a matter of fact, in a different mode from his more well known writing. It had a mill race with the most wonderful ferns growing in the walls, freshened by continual spray. There was a huge house which seemed to have been rebuilt from what might once have been a flour mill, we did not ask. Like Joanna Southcott's house (Rock Cottage), it gave signals of infinite funds, but in this case very loud.

There was every kind of path and flower bed with every kind of flower, which remark might be made truly of Hidcote except that here, the effect was so very different. Here there were places which shouted of secret corners, seats were strategically placed for rests or assignations, and like the other gardens it climbed up slopes, this way and that. It should have been wonderful. MGF had a sour look on his face and I felt a curious disquiet. Very high up those slopes of rich earth there were fruit and vegetable gardens, full of flourishing produce. I was awestruck and envious, one could live on this abundance for months. The beds were laid out meticulously, bordered in miniature apple trees. There were quaint cast-iron signs from, I think I recall correctly, a railway station. There was a seat. We sat. In silence. Bees buzzed around herbs. I wished this garden was mine.

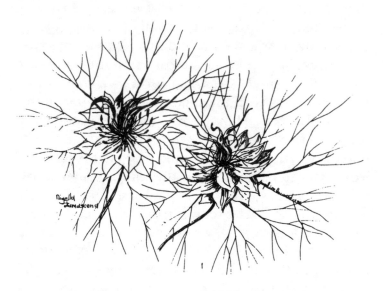

'No you don't,' said MGF. 'If you had all this it wouldn't be like this at all. You'd have samphire and scorzoenera and it would be scruffy but it would taste brilliant just the once a year. And you'd have proper apples not these stage set bonsais, and you wouldn't have those fake bits of iron, you'd have real bits of old iron rusting away probably. I wonder where they buy their bees? 'Smatter of fact I don't think they're real bees, they're holograms.' There was more in this vein, and I began to get his point of

view although by the time he finally sat glowering
quietly, I felt a tender sympathy for the owners. I also
felt very stupid for my earlier reaction. Horticultural
aesthetics are a very serious matter with MGF. He
had highlighted my dim disquiet. The garden had not
been grown over a long period with labour and
struggle and love, it had been imported wholesale
and popped in by experts, or so we decided. To be
kinder, once it had settled down, and if someone
showed a real interest in it, this garden could become
wonderful. All the elements of a perfect country
garden were there, but sometimes a project has all
the right elements, say something at the RSC with a
good play, talented actors, an excellent director and
it just doesn't work.

Perhaps now, after three years, it has all mellowed
and settled in, perhaps time and some other elements
have created a real place out of what was in truth just
an exhibition. Perhaps it was just too new, and a
garden with mature plants should not be new. It will
have the feeling of weird unreality which I experienced at the Chelsea Flower Show, the year that
the Women's Institute won with a cottage garden. I
feel that over such displays (and the W.I. garden was
rather marvellous, like a shot from Howard's End)
hangs that scent of immense quantities of heartless
money shamelessly displayed, like a poisonous mist.

'Come on,' I said to MGF. 'I need a cup of tea.'

So then we had a lovely time being bitchy and
exonerating ourselves generously of self-accusations
of sour grapes (certainly not, I wouldn't have it
given) until we became more positive, after we had
returned home, over a pint or so of beer or was it

draught cider? We mellowed, even as a new garden will mellow. Time is an essential element, and plants are better enjoyed put in one or two at a time, with periods of consideration in between. A fully worked out garden design might be a marvellous work of art, but can never take into consideration the Even Better Idea which occurs later, born out of long looking at effects. I have seen some rather wonderful ideas put rapidly into effect on television this year, by Gay Search and other designers. I have marvelled at the fun these people have going to nurseries and getting four of everything to fill in quickly, and seeing the poppies pop out of gravel just as ordered, and wonderful armchairs created from quite mature box trees supported by expensive iron supports. Great stuff, but what then? The proud owners have nothing to do in the garden except be in it, which to me seems very strange. A garden is for *doing*, not just walking around and sitting in, although that is part of the pleasure. It is never finished, and to create it all in a flash of cash misses almost all the point.

If I ever became feeble in old age, however, and have some spare cash, I would take great pleasure in designing a garden and having helpers to effect the work, and someone with heart and ideas to discuss progress with. That would be very nice; I would have some raised beds so that I could totter along deadheading without too much bending, and frequent seats, each one surrounded by my favourite plants, and my alpines would be on strong eye-level shelves, an idea I consider from time to time as it is, because close inspection is rewarding for tiny flowers. Perhaps in fact I should start such a garden now, rearrange everything I have, because it will take at least ten years to get all of that right.

If you are really wealthy and want to buy into the future and have it now, you can have whole mature trees transplanted. Lorries and cranes will appear, with half a forest. Morning, nothing; evening, a mature woodland.

The trees at Batsford and Sezincote have taken rather longer than that to grow, and I do not believe that such marvellous effects could ever be achieved rapidly. Call me old fashioned.

I so look forward to taking J & G to Sezincote especially, because both of them are deeply interested as I am myself, perhaps surprisingly, in postmodern philosophy which sprang from architecture. The house was the inspiration for the Brighton Pavilion, a unique distinction which I find awe-inspiring. It has been related to me that in the Borchester area there have been instances of racial discrimination against what as a child we knew as Indians, but may now perhaps come also from Pakistan, an important distinction to many. Not English roses, anyway. To these perpetrators of prejudice from mythical English countryside, I would like to point out that what is very possibly the most beautiful country house in England is based firmly in Indian origins. Its details borrow extravagantly from mosque design, but incorporate, perhaps from ignorance or perhaps from an unrecognised forerunner of the post-modern attitude which uses what it will, Hindu elements. Not being a purist, I accept joyfully a marvellous result. This building sits perfectly in English woodland. MGF and I went in autumn, which is the best time for this visit. Again, the day was warm and sunny and we were in high spirits. MGF had been going on at length for some time about this trip and I was fully prepared to be confronted with something arising in his own mind, which alas might remain there. It is less than an hour's drive, however, so not much would be wasted. Off we went.

At Moreton-in-Marsh, the original model for Much Binding in the Marsh, which my older readers will recall with affection from the days when a few mild *double entendres* were considered wildly scandulous, MGF pointed out that Sezincote did not actually officially open for another hour, therefore it might be nice to have a pint. I was driving the car, of course, and he doesn't really give a damn what happens to his chauffeurs. I have spoken of his powers of persuasion. We went into the pub. The sun streamed in through old windows onto a log fire, a double-strength fix of welcoming impressions. I was 'dressed up' somewhat, in my khaki-mud trousers, black shirt, grey waistcoat, silk scarf, black walking boots and large-interesting-lady-writer's-Clint-Eastwood-type hat. I was feeling good, euphoric that my illness was apparently behind me, a day off – heck, why not? Suddenly my spirits rose even further as I sat down in front of a foaming pint of specially selected brew and MGF, sitting down with his usual slow graceful folding action asked all the occupants of the place: 'Oh! Why can't it *always be like this*?' He very nearly got a round of applause, everybody was in a good mood. Indian summer has that powerful effect upon the English, who were lashing into bar curry and scotch chasers like any decent colonial with malaria.

At that supreme moment, nothing was more distant from me than actual gardening, or plants, planting, surroundings. That was to come later. We gossiped on lofty subjects until I suddenly realised that Sezincote was open now, and that I had inadvertently drunk too much to legally drive my car. It is about a half hour's walk, so I ordered us a taxi, inspired with the idea that we were doing things in style, what was cash anyway? We sat in the back, MGF as excited as a child at being the one to reveal the view as we progressed down the drive in aristocratic fashion, under the avenue of magnificent trees. When the copper onion dome finally appeared, he was rewarded with cries of joy from me. I think I heard the taxi-driver scoffing and sneering, firmly in the role of prole despising airy-fairy arty types. He charged me an exorbitant sum. As I paid I surprised him with some gutter invective and MGF and I began our tour with a fit of hysterics. There was nobody about to take our entrance fees, the place seemed completely deserted. The house is only open to the public on infrequent occasions so, feeling guilty (in my case, MGF just shrugged) we began what must be one of the most beautiful autumn afternoons I have ever experienced.

This was not the first time I had experienced the feeling that I had been born in the wrong time and place, but it was the strongest. I was filled with most pure longing to simply live there, and have the privilege of maintaining those glorious trees, walking every day through the water garden which has quite the best design of bridge I have ever seen. To get a closer look at some of the sculptures I walked on the precipitous edge of the pond, something I would usually have avoided, but fear was not going to deny me anything that day. We regretted that some of the trellis work on the balconies of the house needed replacing in a proper style, but this was a tiny quibble; we had more fun praising. The conservatory is wonderfully decayed, and has such a good atmosphere it would perhaps be a shame to restore it. If it was mine I would find a way of preserving it so that it did not rot away, and grow my exotics in the elegance as it now stands. We sat for a long time gazing happily at damp walls, crumbling planters and cracked tiles, all of which was far from depressing. This structure, which is very large and built on a grand curve, makes a reproduction conservatory, however carefully copied, look like something out of a funfair. We were very happy.

It was on that day I was introduced to acers. There is at least one vast acer at Sezincote, and you can stand underneath it and stare up through the exquisite patterns of its leaves until your neck aches, it is so beautiful. I think that tree must be very old, for they grow slowly.

It was also here that MGF suddenly picked up some rotting leaves from under a tree and made me sniff them. Strawberry jam! So by the time we had seen and discussed and contemplated everything including a strangely wonderful building to one side of the main house, the light was fading. We had not seen any other people all afternoon. There was the problem of getting back to Moreton-in-Marsh and there was no telephone for another expensive taxi. We faced what now seemed quite a long walk. Just at that low moment an enormous white limo suddenly appeared as if at a very special wish, and the window rolled down to reveal a very typical aristocratic country gentleman and three vigorous dogs. He offered us a lift up to the main gates; he was the neighbour from across the way, he'd just dropped in but it seemed that everyone was still away. We thoroughly enjoyed being in the back of that splendid vehicle, quietly admiring its cream suede upholstery, and its hand plaited silk tassels. It reminded me of the car of one of my widowed mother's boyfriends, when I was five years old; I had spent hours in such a car in pub car parks, searching diligently for the blue screw of salt in Smith's crisps and being very bored. I was not bored here, and had a rapid fantasy of being invited back to dinner, being fallen in love with, married, filthy rich and having huge parties over at Batsford, for it was none other than the lord of that manor who now kindly chauffered MGF and I. We found ourselves on the main road and legged it back in the dusk, feeling intensely well blessed. Very sadly, we somehow heard that this knight in shining armour had died the following year in a fishing accident. His waders had got filled with water and he had been dragged away by the current. I might have been a wealthy widow! I vulgarly thought.

MGF again forced me to accompany him into the pub but we did not stay long. Moreton-in-Marsh has a main training centre for firemen, and there was a firemen's convention.

These very necessary but over-butch males began to give us hostile glances. MGF has a silky pony-tail halfway down his back and I have described my garb. I think we were labelled 'two weird arty queers' or something of the kind, and when a few remarks were loudly made and one of them made a lunge for my hat (I froze him with one of my looks), we felt it was time to hit the road. I felt sorry for the sole fireman sitting quietly, a gentle soul like a fish out of water; I am sure he and all his colleagues are fearless in the face of a fire, but I could see that he was very wary in that testosterone-and-lager soaked rabble. I later realised that I was the sole female in that pub, and it must have riled them that I was rather too old for them and looked nothing at all like a monstrosity off page three.

This interlude spoiled nothing for us and could never mar the memories of Sezincote. The reverse of the coin showed itself next day when I went out into my little rabbit hole garden. It seemed cramped, pathetic, poverty-stricken. This feeling of failure and misfortune wore off shortly after some strong coffee, breakfast with vitamins, a shower and some fresh clothes. It always does. There's nothing wrong with the garden. Every high must be paid for, and during such times, as I had the day before remembered, I always say 'this too shall pass'. And it does; this is a Sufi method of getting through depression which never fails, but you must always remember to say the magic words at particularly wonderful moments.

I began to warm up to my usual state when out at the back of the house, relishing the softness of the autumn sunshine, imagining the first nips of frost, the scent of bonfires. Autumn. And then of course I snapped out of what was threatening to become a nostalgic mood of slushy sentiment, two more minutes of that I'd start writing a poem about falling leaves! There was a truly immense amount of labour to accomplish, as there always is. As I trimmed and planted bulbs and tidied and rearranged everything, scraping rotting stuff from behind the plantpots and all the other tasks I always find, my spirit expanded. I was very well off again, here in the real world. When tasks are going well and future plans are made, I never need anything except the present moment in the present place. As all gardeners know.

16

Gullibility

A strong imagination and the ability to hope force-
fully are excellent qualities which a gardener must
have. I would have had just a scruffy yard, or at best
a very clean and neat yard at the back of my house if I
had been another sort of person. If you intensify
hope and faith, adventurousness and imagination,
the distorted result can become sheer gullibility. You
will believe whatever you want to believe, and worse,
what others want you to believe about the possi-
bilities of your garden. You will then become the
willing victim of whatever the big business end of
gardening want you to believe. This is so in all areas
of what were once purely domestic survival techniques, cooking, warmth, cleanliness and general
ambience. Can anyone really believe that life cannot
be worth living without new décor annually, or a
complete fitted kitchen looking either like an
operating theatre or a library, according to the latest
persuasions of fashion? Even before all that kind of
nonsense, it was possible, I confess, to be completely
daft without media persuasion.

I am incredulous now at some of the utterly stupid
but marvellous ideas I have had in the past. The
ignorance and naivety I displayed at times are hard
to explain. I am neither ashamed nor regretful,
though. The hard way of learning gardening is less

puritan than it sounds.

I was twenty-two, and the garden I had then was the one where I grew those extremely large sunflowers. They were extraordinary enough but what I originally planned would have had the RHS up there in force, cameras flashing.

I got a book on vegetable gardening out of the library in Sowerby Bridge, and as I read it I began to be totally taken over by a terrible craving to get out there and begin immediately. This was a wonderful book. It showed you how to lay out a vegetable plot, what time of year to plant what and when to expect a harvest. I was so excited people got worried; I speak very fast and my eyes burn when I am enthused and I am sure that this vision I had conceived was off the scale. I have always been attracted to anything different, original or unusual, and in this book there were vegetables I had never even heard of. Now they are commonplace in supermarkets and in Indian corner shops, but then, we were very conservative. The book confidently listed aubergines, sweet peppers, sweetcorn and okra among its kitchen garden essentials, and I visualised it extravagantly. I had recently held my first dinner party at that house, even before we had been able to acquire a table, and it had been a great success. I had served something which no person present had eaten before; jugged hare. I had done it in a pressure cooker, and it was wonderful, but the accompanying vegetables had been carrots, onions and swedes over brown rice. It had still been considered very original and exotic, especially with massive libations of a very successful if unsuitable (this was in the days before everyone lived to eat and do each other down with their wine knowledge) elderflower wine which I had made myself, and the fact that we sat on the floor around a door which I had lifted from its hinges and covered in a white bedsheet and decorated with ivy. I would top that, easily, once my vegetable garden got going.

I took a sheet of drawing paper and lovingly planned everything, rearranging the book's plan to suit the aspects of sun and wind by my stream-side plan. The next thing, of course, was buying seeds.

It was a sad day when Woolworth's failed to provide me with okra seed, and sadder when even the usual small department in an ironmongers had never heard of aubergines. In Halifax in those days you got 'funny looks' for mentioning anything not strictly British, and I give myself full marks for courage in battling on. Eventually I got help from an elderly gardening man who had a wonderful allotment not far from where I lived. I would sometimes take an hour to visit him and we would sit smoking, he a pipe and me my licorice-paper rollies, and he would pass on a lot of his knowledge. Here it was that I learned such gems as 'always plant your nasturtiums on the 1st of May'. If I plant them before then, which you can easily do this much further south and with the warmer climate, I feel guilty and endangered. Everything he told me was true enough, for that time and place. Including the fact that the book I had got from Sowerby Bridge library was an American gardening book, and from New Orleans, further-more. My sadness was deep, and he was kind enough not to laugh. Thank God that MGF was not in my life at that time; I would never have recovered from his contempt.

I did manage to grow some very excellent parsnips, Welsh onions and some parsley besides lots of flowers. Now the climate is changing, I know quite a few people, most of them Jamaican, who successfully grow sweetcorn, various hot peppers and other interesting herbs in back gardens. I myself once grew seven female specimens of a very interesting herb in a back garden, and the photograph of me standing by them with a proudly dreamy smile shows that I do not exaggerate their height at over ten feet tall. That was a good summer, but part of the success was due to some advice I was given on feeding. Molasses should be dissolved and fed to the plants weekly; this makes for strong healthy plants with a fine flavour. I keep meaning to try this on other plants. I do not waste space with large interesting herbs in this tiny place, there really is no room. I am too taken up with planting other impossible dreams, some of them inspired by catalogues full of sheer lies.

Most descriptions of flowers in seed and plant catalogues exaggerate wildly. 'Flowers fifteen centimetres across' refers to 'flowers seven centimetres across with one or two larger ones if you are lucky'.

'Covering a bank with its masses of flowers' means 'might be quite a nice little plant even in its first year, but you will have to wait for flowers'.

'Three to four metres with exotic blooms' means 'one metre and straggly, probably won't survive the winter outside'.

'Rapid ground cover' means with the weeds you thought you had taken out, not with this miraculous new variety of carpeting rose/gardenia/penstemon/ giant cyclamen, which may or may not get its roots in, but will grow slowly and uncertainly.

'Slow growing tree' means growth is imperceptible, and as it arrived only fifteen centimetres tall, five years ago, you wonder if eighteen quid was rather expensive.

'Glorious blue' means 'mucky sort of mauve'.

'Prolific flowerer' is the one you still do not know what causes the buds to drop off before opening.

It is not only catalogues which are guilty of this gross misinformation. On television recently I witnessed an expert in passifloras state than most of more than a hundred varieties would thrive in most parts of the British Isles. Is he kidding, or what? In a greenhouse, perhaps, but on the Scottish moorlands, high in the Pennines, or on a windswept coast, I truly doubt this. Such disappointments the gullible are in for, how sad. How sad too when people with not much money and a wild desire to have a lovely garden are conned out of some of their resources for a golden dream. Isn't it possible to make a living out of plants by telling the truth? But as I have described, sometimes the impossible can be achieved, so it is a case of *caveat emptor*. I still read some of these descriptions with chagrin, knowing that failure will be the inevitable result for many people. We are often simply not told that some of those plants must overwinter in a greenhouse, often a heated green-house. Only with more experience and acquisition of knowledge will you avoid spending money on something doomed to failure.

'Most parts of Britain' is likely to mean Cornwall or even the Scilly Isles with some of these South African bulbs which are sold in garden centres lately, and which to the untutored eye appear to be as easy as crocuses. Several of them if they come up at all will only do so once in most parts of Britain, and most of them have special requirements. How many gardens have you been in where there was a thriving patch of ixias for example? Or canna lilies? Or babiana? The writers of the information on the packs are economical with the truth, to say the least.

It is surprising how naive new gardeners can be. J, for example, honestly wondered why a packet of seeds contained a hundred and fifty seeds. 'Seems a lot, I shan't need so many, shall I?' The reason is that you are lucky to get two per cent germination with many things, and that if you get more than you want, you can weed them out, and indeed have to. To get full germination and rear every plant is rare indeed, even perhaps for professionals. Generally speaking, with a very small space it is better and cheaper to buy small plants than try to raise from seed, and for all the dozens of wonderful seeds available, you need a greenhouse to try more than one or two varieties. I try one or two different ones every year now. Last winter I started off some Chinese lanterns, with weirdly enough, one hundred per cent germination, but painfully slow growth. The packet never even hinted that it would take two years before I saw any flowers. I gave a lot of them to a plant sale for a worthy cause, so if you have room for lots of little pots cluttering up windowsills and paths then go ahead, it can be good fun. It is not really more economical. The cost of a packet of seeds is quite high now, and a propagator, heated or not, is another expense, plant labels, and time and space are all involved. If you have plenty of both of the two last named, you may have success. It is thrilling to watch seeds germinate and grow successfully, but windowsills are likely to encourage weedy growth. Hardening off can be lengthy and heart- and back-breaking chasing in and out with trays of plants as the weather changes. And then to find that the final result is, through a magnifying glass, slightly like the illustration on the packet . . .?

Still, I am the one who has vowed to grow a banana tree, so you may smile at my dire warnings. Take risks by all means, but be prepared to be exasperated when yet again your tree fern spores come to nothing. 'One of the Globe's most ancient life forms, reaches ten metres or more, exotic shape' etc., etc. Gosh, you think, must have at least one of those, and what marvellous presents they would make. Certainly would.

As would have my surplus home-grown okra and bell peppers. These days, in this sheltered hollow, it could just be possible to grow these things, but more for fun than necessity. It is a very short walk to two excellent Indian corner shops, after all.

The sheer lies on plant labels and seed packets will not deceive anyone who has long experience, many books to hand and all the right conditions for growing, but I do feel sorry for the newly enthused gardener with not much spare cash. This is just one more good reason why we must exchange all our information. Gardeners love to do this, I have discovered.

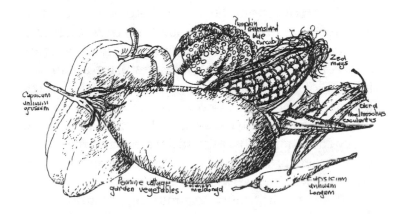

It was MGF who first said to me that gardeners were the only truly classless society, and that they were all nice people. We were in Mill Street Garden, in Warwick at the time, and I had just had the privilege of being introduced to its owner, a very pleasant retired doctor of advanced years. For this man nothing is too much trouble if it is to do with plants. He has his garden open to the public a great deal of the time, and seekers after truth are always welcome. He loves to fetch a reference book if on a rare occasion he cannot immediately answer a query, and his enthusiasm is infectious. The result of this attitude shows in his marvellous garden by the river, under the battlements of Warwick Castle. He changes the plan for some beds every year, using an exquisite colour sense to offer an exciting display to his frequent visitors. His are the best towers of sweet peas I have ever seen, gloriously lush and crammed with flowers. In early spring his crown imperial fritillaries are matchless, and it was here that I first caught my passion for sempervivums, for he has an excellent collection. His woodland shade area is excellent. On his open days, he is often to be found sitting outside continually chatting with visitors about plants, or perhaps telling stories about the history of his house, or the cheeky swans which invaded his kitchen.

I have found this open and friendly attitude in every gardener I have ever spoken to, and they are a very varied group of people. People who in other contexts would gaze at the ceiling with an icy little smile are to be found communing intensely with people who in yet other contexts would possibly be heard uttering curses about *bourgeoisie* and so on. Everything except the fascination of plants gets forgotten, and great friendships are formed, across large age gaps too. And the world of gardening is also one inhabited quite as much by females as males, and in no way will any true gardener patronise a female gardener. I do so like all this. You can always tell when you are being classified according to the way you dress and cut your hair and so on, but I have never once seen any gardener even notice the tattoo on my left wrist, whereas within minutes of meeting just about everyone else will mention it. We gardeners are not trivial, judgemental people. The exchange of information, plants, advice, seeds and cuttings is enthusiastic. So it is rather sad when we read legends on plant labels and in seed catalogues which are unlikely to bear much relation to reality. Perhaps professional advertisers and salespeople write this stuff, but who allows it? People who must once have delighted in plants, were trained in horticulture. Our defence against all this fantasy must be more knowledge, as in everything.

Taste is another matter, but this too can be manipulated. I can not believe that anyone would purchase, of their own free will, a lumpy animal sculpture with glass eyes, and then put it in the garden where it can be seen.

If you are the kind of person who really believes that a built-in hob and a fan assisted oven and a rack of odd gadgets like a torturer's toy-box will make you into a better cook, you are probably even now purchasing fake stepping-stones with images of squirrels stamped into them. Or in danger of spending enough money to feed and clothe an entire African village on a brand new fake antique pump, apparently in need of mending as it pours water continually into an imitation half beer barrel. Personally I'd rather have the African village complete with drums in my garden, just so long as their water supply did not come from something as ugly as the above-described. Same goes for wishing wells. And plant containers with imitation brick or basketwork markings. In Greece they put geraniums in large tin cans sometimes painted blue, and we would do better to copy this on two counts; they look better and recycle garbage.

I have never had a garden gnome, but sometimes I think that a particularly vulgar or horrible one might be displayed, to annoy those with good taste (I have a wicked streak) but it would soon annoy me too much. Years ago Eduardo Paolozzi filled the front garden of his London home with six-foot gnomes, and this I have to approve of, it has style. It is those nasty little ones which bother me, detracting from the flowers, grinning eternally and endorsing the popular view that art is incomprehensible. Such things all belong in a museum of kitsch, and if you can think in the long term I advise you to buy as many as possible of these ghastly garden ornaments and hide them away for thirty years. This way nobody needs to see them and you will make a fortune in your old age. Possibly even now there are people doing just this. They are the same people who kept the sunburst mirrors, the artist's palette coffee table, the oil-filled dreamy bubble lamp, the Clarice Cliff wall masks, the crinoline lady tablecloth brushes and telephone covers, the weird lamp bases and other objects inspired by models of atoms. Some maybe yes, maybe no, but let us be frank here; most bird-baths in garden centres are an insult to birds. Can you tell the time by a sundial? Can you find a sundial worth possessing?

The only garden sculptures worth having are genuine antiques, and these of course will be instantly stolen and be on the ship to America before your coffee is brewed in the morning. There is a big market for such things, including good garden furniture. I have mentioned this before. If you want your garden to resemble a not-very-nice country pub then get some white resin furniture, not forgetting an umbrella with orange roses. You will be blinded by the reflection of light so get a pair of the naffest sunglasses you can find at the same time, as a disguise. You don't want your friends knowing you would buy such stuff. The dark khaki green is marginally better; wood is best. Iron looks wonderful, especially the excellent reproduction objects appearing in National Trust gardens, but is rather expensive. My bench cost twenty pounds. Director's chairs are fine. Anything else is out of the question. Plants are the point of a garden, and objects which scream for visual attention will get it, and your pleasant terracotta and glazed pots will disappear.

Hanging baskets are suspect. I have had several, and in themselves they are not bad, creating more space in which to grow things, and hiding dull bits of wall. But I have been sitting and looking slowly at my rabbit hole this hot summer, and wondering if something which needs watering twice a day even with gel crystals in the compost, and which in windy weather circles around making the narcissus and me quite dizzy and in dry weather gets easily crisped, and which hangs off an ugly black fake wrought iron bracket, and which is very heavy to hang, an enormous bother to plant, and which produces its best flowers up high where I can't see them . . .? They can be prevented from swinging about by discreet wiring, but then they are not hanging. Those metal manger-type are quite good when they are filled with exotic begonias, but until the foliage covers their stuffing, they too look ugly. Try to put them so that taller plants in containers at least partially cover them until they look presentable. They help down a rabbit hole where sweeping tracts of land are hard to find. On no account have plantpots clinging to drainpipes, however, they resemble the worst kind of municipal floral display. Next will come the fairy lights, and then you have not a garden but a bad grotto.

So I am being opinionated and giving advice. Where did I get this trait from? Well, I blame MGF entirely, with regard to gardens. He is so full of strong opinions and gives advice continually, to everyone he meets, that I could not but have become more aware of what choices I was making, not only with regard to plants, but to all the other things in the garden. I have him to thank for pouring scorn on my long ago idea of painting all the brickwork and woodwork blinding white in order to reflect light and show off my flowers.

'Soon looks tacky, like white tee-shirts my dear, looks as if you've been to bloody Benidorm for your hols, reflects the light as much into your eyes as onto the plants. Cream on the cemented wall, dark green for the gate. Nothing else will do.' He was right; it is a Victorian house after all. I had nurtured a horror of 'garden-gate green' all my life, and I do not know why. Perhaps in some unhappy bit of my childhood, when all garden gates were dark green, I was shut in behind one in a state of misery. But that has worn off, because behind my traditional green gate I am truly happy. Now, dark blue is in fashion for fences and gates. This is tempting. It is not exactly the Greek blue which looks so good on Greek islands, nor is it the Indian light blue which I expended so much energy getting rid of when I came here, and which never looks anything but awful, anywhere, but a rich indigo sort of colour. This just might be acceptable if I get around to repainting. The weird fuchsia pink on the back of S's gate is a mystery, I think she probably did that (had it done) for some spiritual reason. You notice this colour more than anything else when you look down that end of her garden, and the silver-painted latches and hinges do not improve matters. If I did anything like that here, in so small a space, I would soon break down and start trembling. Be very careful what you take into your small garden, even more careful than in your living-room indoors. A garden is a very special place, and must envelop you in harmonious feelings the moment you step outside.

To begin to float into a good mood in your garden and then be smacked in the eye with a piece of rotting fat placed there for birds is not good. Get rid of it immediately, and those nasty bags of nuts. Put them, if you must, where not only cats cannot get the birds but where humans cannot walk into them, or see them dangling sadly in rainy weather, suppurating away like some victim hanging in chains in Warwick Castle. They probably dangle, unhygienic and foul, off your washline. I got rid of my washlines, tucking just one in out of sight to be brought out only occasionally. Washing blocks light from plants. Since I did not have those awful blue plastic lines everything looks more spacious out there. I have not given in and bought a rotary. I am immune to all sales-talk. I shall never be caught out by the barbecue craze, barbecues scorch plants. The garden is not about things like that. It is about growth, and awe and mystery, about beauty and peace.

In a novel by Mary McCarthy there is a character

who takes his sole pot plant for a walk every day. I like people like that. Also, I once saw a short French movie about a very old poverty stricken woman who put some dried beans to soak for her dinner, and when one sprouted, she planted it on her window-sill. Eventually it grew too big for its pot so she too took her plant for a walk, and when nobody was looking, transplanted it into the middle of a border of splendid plants in the public gardens. This is what gardening is about, no matter how small a space of earth you have. I feel very fortunate here.

I have room to go outside and commune with around a hundred and fifty of my closest friends. And every one has an extension into my thoughts, of where I first heard of it, saw it, and wanted it.

I seem to have put more of my energies and resources into this odd little space than into anything else for seven years. And the returns are infinite.

Appendices

Chapter 1

You have been warned. If you become seriously interested in plants then everything else will have less meaning. A life without holidays, sex, regular cooked meals and a trivial social life (i.e. other people not interested in plants) will be your lot. However, days out to other gardens, passionate friendships (with other people interested in plants), sustaining snacks eaten with earthy hands and washed down with alcohol after sunset will enhance a life now filled with meaning.

Get a Gardening Friend who knows a great deal more than you. These may be obtained by sheer luck, or through various horticultural societies, for example The Hardy Plant Society, Secretary: Mrs Pam Adams, Little Orchard, Great Comberton, nr. Pershore, Worcs WR10 3DP. Also, visit the shows at the Royal Horticultural Society. You will soon be deep in conversation with complete strangers who will give you their addresses and a great deal of good advice.

Never trust a heavy drinker, who thinks that flowers are the splodges of colour in pub gardens, to water your plants when you are away for a few days.

Winter is not around Christmas it is when a sustained cold period occurs. You must cultivate your instincts and keep up with the climatic changes. There is no longer a ritual of garden jobs for each month, you can do almost any job at any time of year – so long as you choose the right time for the plant and the weather. No worries here, it comes to you like knowing when to make love, if you are truly in love.

Do not copy other people's ideas of what a beautiful garden should be. Your garden is an expression of your own soul, limited only by space, and then not much. Your garden is where you can most become yourself, and a voyage of continual serendipity is ahead.

Chapter 2

Never clear an overgrown patch by poisoning or burning. It only works for a short while and you could have serious trouble to follow. Dig or black it out for a while, or start gradually, a couple of square yards at a time, but never think that a huge clean sweep is best. Take a look at the Sahara if you do not believe this.

Do not use peat. Even if it were ecologically viable, it disappears quickly. First study your plant, and its needs, and then supply those needs in a way which

232

does not destroy another piece of earth.

Snails cannot read English. Try Latin.

Chapter 3

All clematis require alkaline soil.
All rhododendrons require acid soil, and are a menace. Some clematis will grow on a north-facing wall – but they will climb over the wall and flower for the neighbour. How generous are you?

Stop bothering with houseplants unless you have absolutely no earth of your own outside. Two houseplants in one house are plenty – you will need all the windowsills for cuttings and trays of seeds.

Jasmine, Virginia creeper and *Clematis montana* grow very quickly, but in a small space they will soon create an impenetrable jungle and you will then learn how to be a ruthless fascist.

Only grow plants which you love, or else grow to love the plants you have got. Always consult plant-minded friends and the huge RHS books or similar tomes of information before planting anything. No good putting a shade plant in full sun, is it?

Beware all exotic-seeming space fillers foisted onto you by well meaning people.

Yes, cats can find earth under groundcover plants. Dead patches will reveal where.

Chapter 4

Go and visit great gardens, small gardens, gardens in the NGS Yellow Book. Look carefully at every plant, note where it is growing, and then go home and get one and put it in a totally different environment. Sometimes it works, and is a lot more fun than skiing, going to a theme park, go-karting, making lasagne or consuming the contents of bottles labelled 'Drink Me'. Well, this last is close.

If anyone else helps you by doing your garden, then you have lost it, even if you pay them for a few hours a week. Give up your career and get down there yourself.

Most modern roses are worth less than the soil they are planted in. Screw up brightly coloured rubbish and pin it to dead bushes to obtain the same effect without the problem of aphids.

Almost anything can be grown in a pot. Not always forever, but for a long and interesting time. Palm trees, bananas, climbing roses, lilies, acers, *Rhus typhina*, bamboo all do well in pots. Impress yourself: try anything – after discovering its needs. Pots are wonderful, you can play at rearranging the entire garden several times a day if you like.

Gardening is a complete therapy for all manner of blues, and for a lot of physical torments as well. Familiarise yourself with the principles of the wheel, the lever, and the big strong man, wear a body-belt around your lower back, take it slowly and learn to lift properly without exception.

Beware of strange laughter in the shrubbery.

Chapter 5

If you have a very shady garden, there are two courses of action. Study shade plants and create something wonderful with them, or remove an unwanted source of shade if possible. Find out about a tree before cutting it down, some are precious and some are expendable, sometimes.

Gardening in the Shade by Margery Fish is a classic and excellent book which will help you, and the RHS book always indicates if a plant prefers shade, or half-shade. Do not forget that 'shade' does not mean total darkness under a greedy conifer, and that 'half-shade' usually means something more like 'more than half-sunny'. Many things will grow in deep shade but will be tall and will bend hungrily towards the light, for example lilies. If you are prepared for this and to support them then why not try them? Much depends upon other factors and you might have a great success. Or a lily graveyard.

Cats and plants look wonderful on postcards. In real life cats pee on plants and kill them. Try to retrain your cat to use a cat-tray in a garden shed or outhouse, and also experiment with wide-mesh chicken wire as a guard around and between plants.

In my experience nothing else will work except a large hungry cat-hating dog, and these dig holes in your garden.

The very best plant food for clematis is cat ashes, but be prepared for ghostly visitations along with the increased flowers.

Procumbens mortei, a Latin term describing certain plants which you still believe will revive when the season changes.

Discuss the shrubs and garden designs of your locale on the way *back* from the off-licence.

MGF has demanded justice with regard to my remark on his powers of weeding, so here be reparation. He speaks eloquently upon the joys of weeding, and weeding as an art form. To remove only destructive weeds and to allow non-destructive weeds is an art, as is the defining of the term 'weed'. Weeding is a satisfying and joyful task, and MGF certainly does not dislike it. Okay?

Chapter 6

Moss, lichen, seed pods are all part of the visual effect of your garden, and not always something which must be got rid of. Too much tidiness results in a sterile effect, and to your dismay you might find that some 'weeds' were prettier than some of your precious flowers. Never garden to impress other

236

people but to satisfy something in yourself.

Sometimes you have to make major sacrifices in order to get in and out of your house. Be prepared for grief as well as joy, and for realising how much you enjoy getting rid of something which has put its entire existence into growing for you. Learning gardening is learning about yourself so if you find yourself continually killing things, consider adding another activity to your life as well as gardening. This should be something needing controlled violence which does no harm, such as karate, clay pigeon shooting or cushion punching.

Simon's garden is progressing: he has dug out wavy-edged flower beds and is planting clematis and so on, he has *got* the message. He now likes moss, even.

Chapter 7

Patience is a virtue, often found in a woman, seldom in a man, but always in a gardener who has learned the hard way.

Flotation tanks have nothing on a hot bath with a drink to hand after a really hard day's gardening. For that Buddha smile, add rosemary and lavender to the water, and make the drink a large one.

Make a note of everything including the composition of the compost and feeding of every pot in your garden. This way you will learn that the reason the bulbs come up the wrong colour or not at all is always inevitable.

Chapter 8

Get a season ticket to Kew; expect everything except miracles.

Listen at all times to good advice, but remember that radical changes to plant environments are better effected during daylight hours after careful thought.

Frost kills plants more easily if they are in containers. It is not just the leaves which suffer and may reappear in spring to Walt Disney music, but the roots, bulbs, corms and tubers. Anything which you would like to try to overwinter outside, in spite of every source informing you that it is not possible, may survive if you securely wrap the pot in bubble plastic, raise it off the cold patio, and swathe all the top growth in agricultural fleece, bought by the yard at garden centres. This last material can be washed and reused several times and is very useful. It makes your garden look as if you are an artist deriving inspiration from Cristo. It can also be used just at night during a period of hardening off plants which you have overwintered indoors, in those years when May never comes and you are sick to death of the indoors looking like a not-very-good garden centre. Clip it to tops of pots, chains on baskets and so on with clothes pegs.

238

Hope is not just a word; it works. But even hope cannot raise the dead.

I have recently again visited Kew, and there, flourishing, was the Mystery Plant. It was at the front of a border, indoors, and a different place. I took a couple of hours making as detailed a drawing of it as possible, and failed quite badly to convey the peculiar delicacy of its stamens, but at least got a fair representation of it generally, and reacquainted myself with what I thought might be a figment. The name of the plant is *Eucnidia grandiflora*, of the laosacea, and it comes from Mexico. There is a warning on it about its stinging leaves. Can't say that either MGF or I noticed that, but I did not touch it again to find out.

Chapter 9

Creating an acid bed with loads of peat is not only non-ecological, it could be fatal. Better to improve the soil you already have.

Acid-loving plants are often blue-flowered. Most of them will not survive in limey soil. It is a waste of time and money to try, but you will.

Blue cordyalis is well worth trying, as some of them are not fussy as to soil, will thrive in shade and do well in pots. A plant in full flower is among the most beautiful sights in the world.

Snails can be kept out of pots if you smear the outer rims thickly with Vaseline. MGF thinks this may be the chemical which revolts snails, but I think they just slide off, as if trying to climb a greasy pole. They also dislike walking across grit, so put a mulch around vulnerable stems.

Try growing clear yellow flowers next to clear blue, the effect is quite eery and wonderful.

Chapter 10

Lust and greed play a large part in gardening. 'Less is more' comes from an aspect of wisdom unknown to gardeners unless they practise Zen.

Alpines in shallow containers take up a lot of floor space: had I thought of starting the garden with them I would have first put in super-strong shelves on the outside walls of the house. This is an idea worth consideration if you have already developed a passion for this very wonderful type of plant.

Finding more space for more plants is a true test of ingenuity, more taxing than a jigsaw, and may well delay the onset of mental decay; it is impossible to stop thinking about this kind of problem until it is solved, at which point you discover another plant to crave.

Since carting compost up a stepladder as described, a growing medium called Grodan has come to my notice. It is special lightweight stuff for roof gardens, so I cannot be the only gardener barmy enough to wish that sky hooks were more than a concept. I have not yet tested it but it certainly sounds worth trying.

No idea is too large or too ambitious for a tiny garden. It is possible to be too sensible (i.e. boring) for your own good. My banana seeds did not even germinate, but this winter I intend to try again using a little propagator.

Chapter 11

Gardens are at their best in the rain; the plants can almost be heard to sing and the colours intensify. Public gardens are not so crowded in the rain. Watering is not necessary. Snails can easily be detected. Ferns love it. Fish love it. As a keen gardener, you love it.

Gardens are places in which to fantasise. You can legitimately be Lord or Lady Muck for a while, and sometimes even dress up for the occasion. Try on straw hats in secret before going out in them, however, they can look very silly.

Water gardens are a big number, but a small fountain is most certainly going to appear down my rabbit hole next spring. The electrical part of the work should be undertaken by a properly qualified electrician, even Versailles is not worth dying for.

Chapter 12

If you garden for money, for another person, stick to the designing and advice. It is an unalterable truth that anyone employing someone else to do their labouring for them immediately turns into a brainless inconsiderate idiot. As all labourers know. Doing the garden of someone too sick to do their own, for no pay, is quite a different matter, and if this opportunity comes your way and you can spare some time, do it. In this case, the owner of the garden is right, no matter what, and only the gentlest of advice can be offered.

There is no such thing as a wild garden.

I think it very possible for a person to become so identified with a garden that their life will be prolonged in order to prevent anyone else getting their hands on it.

The contents of pots can make the character of your tiny garden change radically every year, if you like. Fabulously vulgar giant begonias will flower mightily in strong shade, or you can expect less exotic flowers but wonderful scent from the taller old-fashioned white nicotiana. One year you can have all lilies, flowering at different seasons, and one fine year you can have them all, in case one type of plant fails. Chocolate cosmos, vanilla heliotrope, incense passion, purple petunia stronger and more wonderful than any bottled scent, honeysuckle and nicotiana, after dark, all wafting out at the same time as you wander down the path with a glass of chilled white wine, this unearthly experience can easily be yours. Prepare for hours drifting by as you sit by candlelight on warm evenings, late nights of heavenly peace and satisfaction.

Chapter 13

People will ask you questions about your plants and not listen to the answers. Answer them anyway, it is good practice in remembering names of plants. Always quote the botanical, the common and any nickname you know for the plant, its medicinal properties if any, its country of origin and any other information you may have. That person will either be very interested and start learning for themselves, or they will shut up.

It is very satisfying to give good advice to people and have them ignore it with predictable results. To resist remarking on this requires strong character bringing more satisfaction. You may well grieve for their failed plants, but it is not worth a nervous breakdown; you did what you could. Conversely, if you do not heed good advice and things go wrong – chuck it out and get something from the garden centre.

Spring bulbs growing up through alpines are a nice idea until their flowers are over, and then the leaves hang around for months, looking a mess and shading your alpines. The choice is yours but I now have alpine-only containers.

Some marvellous effects of space can be achieved with mirrors. I plan to search junkshops for cheap old mirrors rather than spend lots of cash on new special waterproofed mirror, because I suspect that none of it will last many years. Maybe yes, maybe no, but it is an exciting idea. Mirrors will also reflect light onto the backs of yearning plants, and enhance the illusion of worlds within worlds in even a very tiny space.

Chapter 14

Aphids cannot be encouraged and ladybirds must be encouraged. Roseclear used as sparingly as possible will get rid of the worst of a sudden infestation without killing lacewings and bees. But aphids are such gross breeders and wonderful survivors, and so practising overkill techniques will not help in the end. Try to assist natural processes. (Doing utterly nothing about aphid infestation will result in the loss of most of your flowers; one can be a bit too Green.)

It was 1976 when we were buried in ladybirds. Come home ladybirds, all is forgiven!

Spiders are good, except for those nasty foreign poisonous things.

Snails, like the poor, are always with us. You will get an unnaturally large number in a small walled garden with pots and other hidey-holes, so a certain amount of unnatural ridding may be permitted, in my opinion. You may decide to tolerate every living thing, but goodbye all your succulent stalks.

If petunias get the mosaic virus, do not handle one after another or you will infect other plants. All members of the solanaceae are susceptible to this, which means tomatoes as well.

If you find flatworms, place in a sealed container and telephone the biology department of your nearest university. If they don't want it, someone may know of a research programme which does. Meanwhile, looking under stones for flatworms will keep you busy and in a ferment of fear and misery. Perhaps during the time-lapse between my writing this not very helpful passage and your reading it, a method of control will have been found. I certainly hope so.

Never never kill an earthworm. Earthworms are *wonderful*.

Get rid of your lawn; compost it as you take it up, in between layers of other waste material, or, if you soaked it in weedkiller, of a type which is not truly inert after use, the lawn must be taken away to the dump where it belongs. Now you can begin to really design a garden, create paths, beds, borders. Put your lawnmower up for sale very soon, because next year there will be hundreds for sale, and the second-hand price will be very low. Try a specimen lawn in a shallow ten-inch container and place on it a mini-ature sundial. Do not bother to mow it if you have a cat, it will be eaten gratefully.

Study the water needs of specimen plants; chances are that you are overwatering, just like you did with that expensive aspidistra.

Put rubber tops on all garden canes, they are dangerous and more so in a small space.

Y-stakes are a brilliant invention. Information from: Davies Systems, Brandsby Lodge, Brandsby, York YO6 4SJ

Too many gadgets in the garden, as in the kitchen, are the sign of an amateur, and some of them will finish up stored away with the food processor, the rice steamer and that awful slow-cooker which filled the house with a smell like boiling compost. An old knife with a short blade is a marvellous thing.

Chapter 15

Every year buy a copy of the Yellow Book, the handbook of the National Garden Society, or the Good Gardens Guide: they are keys to happy days out. The best way to visit gardens is with someone who knows more than you, and the second-best way is to go with someone who knows less than you. This last arrangement is very good for your ego, but it is also a way of refreshing and testing what you have learned. If you totally forget the name of a plant more than four times in an afternoon then you are not doing so well, and will wonder about Alzheimer's and if it might be a good idea to take another course of Gingko, it worked last time. Or you could say you are exhausted, which you will be, and suggest tea, always popular. MGF always suggested the pub, even more popular, but best avoided if you are driving. Indeed, I avoid MGF if I am driving, these days, it is just too hazardous.

Atmosphere is the most important element in a garden. A lawn with low bright borders next to a wire fence does not have atmosphere, or to be exact, it does; sad and bleak.

Garden visiting includes your fantasies of land-owning and creativity on a grand scale. I think we should be quite frank about this as it is completely harmless. It does not cripple your more usual style with, for example, dishonest taxi-drivers, I find. Dressing up for the part is fun too, and long skirts and pony-tails being common of late makes this fairly unobtrusive. I have only once been frankly laughed at, in the garden at Upton. I was wearing a long floaty cotton dress and a large shady straw hat on a blazing hot day. The youth who guffawed was wearing tight purple cycling shorts, big black boots, a frankly filthy tee-shirt and bleached hair and earrings. Life is very strange.

Money is not everything, which is good because however much you have got, or not got, most of it will go on the garden if you become addicted. In gardening as in life, not showing off gets superior results.

Tiny gardens like tiny rooms need to be kept clean and tidy. Rooms can look lived in rather than blitzed, I am always saying to MGF.

Conservatories are not rather public spare bedrooms or uncomfortable dining-rooms where insects fall into your food. Neither are they made from white plastic. Conservatories are for growing tender plants and were never meant for back gardens of small houses, where the proportions are invariably wrong. The best conservatories are rather old and magical, and if you have a creaking flaking old lean to in the back of your small terrace-house, be glad. Someday it will be a listed building.

I think that not only are the firemen getting younger, but that they are wonderful.

Never get into a fast-running stream over your wellie-tops.

Never compare your own garden to some other, more wonderful garden. This is like comparing your latest landscape sketch to a Constable, it just creates despair. Also, Constable is dead.

Sezincote has recently been extensively renovated, I discovered on my last visit. Everything there is marvellous, nothing is spoiled.

Chapter 16

If it costs a lot of money in a garden centre, you will probably be better off without it.

Do not believe everything you read, but read everything about gardening that you can lay your hands on. Having acquired some basic knowledge of the requirements of plants, you are ready to be ambitious, to dream, and will still be conned by catalogues. Never mind, those triple-flowered gorgon's head dianthus would have swamped your pure and simple osteospermum.

Gardeners are the true classless society, but can be rather snobbish about the varieties of plants you grow. One year white gardens or invisible flowers are in, the next it is amazingly hot borders. Take no damn notice, these are the same people who leapt upon Britain's first pizza and became secretly addicted; although they burble about sushi and arcane types of Mexican chilli, we know what they send out for in the night.

If you really and truly adore garden gnomes and reconstituted stone nightmares I still do not advise you to have them in a small garden. Start up in business for yourself and sell them to other people. Keep your garden beautiful. Colours of paintwork and garden furniture is important, but the greatest beautifier, indeed its source of life, is light. Flower colours glow at dusk and this is the best time to walk down there and marvel. High noon is bleached out, this is when the plants get lots of energy so you can leave them to it most days. After dark is very special. Candles in glass jars, or carefully placed on canes with paper shades are the best light, but could in dry weather set fire to the house via a dry creeper. I am very wary of this. Last week I went to a party to celebrate a garden, not more than twice the size of my own, and the owner had got a set of fix-them-yourself low wattage lamps in globes. I think that these are undoubtedly the best design of garden light I have seen; she had placed one where it illuminated the underside of a tree, for example, and the effect was perfect. They currently cost £39.00 from Great Mills, who incidentally have the cheapest and nicest glazed clay pots.

Light and its effects is an art form, and you can have fun with this yourself. If you sit quietly out there at different times of day or night, just looking at your plants, ideas will come. Before you paint your fence blue, or some other interesting colour, look at it by candlelight, electric light, sunlight and daylight.

Even if you get some good electric lamps, to sit outside with just one or two candles and a glass of wine on a warm still night, with stars overhead and the scents heavy around you is an experience that everyone should have. Even the tiniest yard can be transformed, and transformed again.

As a matter of fact, I am wrestling with some entirely new ideas for my rabbit hole. Can it possibly be that I am about to start it all over again?